"Leaders in every walk of life should be reading this book. This is disaster at its worst; solutions and leadership at its best."

R.P. – Education Administrator

"Your book ties the dots together in leadership substance while everyone in the civilian world talks about organization and framework. Great book and an easy read."

Captain, U.S. Marine Corps

"What is taught in the book should be easily applied to normal day-to-day leadership skill-building initiatives. Your viewpoints will provide beneficial reviews to numerous corporate and government emergency procedures and processes."

J.F. – Business Owner and former
US Government employee

"People think in abstract terms before a disaster, but when the crisis comes, those abstracts kick into reality. This book deals with reality from experience. We can program ourselves to respond quickly and professionally by looking at the lessons of the past and being ready to apply them to the present."

P.S. – 35+ years Communication
Professional & Newspaper Editor

"This book is a quick and easy guide for those that think "it" will never happen to you or your organization, and if it does, how you can be prepared. You will surprise yourself with what you can actually do to lead, if you are ready."

B.P. – Disaster Response Leader

Leadership When The Sky Falls

LEADERSHIP LESSONS
FROM THE SHUTTLE
COLUMBIA DISASTER

Robert Hurst

authorHOUSE®

AuthorHouse™
1663 Liberty Drive, Suite 200
Bloomington, IN 47403
www.authorhouse.com
Phone: 1-800-839-8640

First published by AuthorHouse 3/11/2008

ISBN: 978-1-4343-6107-3 (sc)

Printed in the United States of America
Bloomington, Indiana

This book is printed on acid-free paper.

DEDICATION

This book is dedicated to people from several walks of life:

- To my wonderful wife for being the energy and inspiration that keeps me going. You are truly a Proverbs 31 woman.

- To each of my wonderful children who are leaders within their own spheres of influence. The leadership journey is never ending; continue on and finish strong!

- To the Nacogdoches, Texas, leadership team who labored long hours under intense scrutiny and pressure during those first days of the space shuttle Columbia disaster. You were awe-inspiring and did a magnificent job!

- To the thousands of volunteers in emergency services throughout East Texas who serve their community selflessly in times of crisis. Your sacrifice is appreciated.

- To the men and women of the NASA astronaut corps. Your calm courage during a time of personal and professional tragedy was an anchor amidst the storm of response.

- Finally, to the seven astronauts who lost their lives on February 1, 2003. Your mission became our mission.

ACKNOWLEDGEMENTS

This project never would have been completed without the able assistance and input of several people. My daughter became the best writing assistant there is and I certainly needed the help putting my thoughts into words. Louellen, you have a gift; continue with it. Regina Story became the print editor I desperately needed to get the i's dotted, the t's crossed, and proper English used in all the right places. She is also my mother and probably never thought she would be using a lifetime of English teaching and print editing for one of her own. Thanks for the help, mother. Finally, my wife, my partner and best friend for all these years, continually kept up the encouragement to put my experiences on paper and believed in me enough to keep urging me onward when I needed it the most. Without these, and a cast of characters in the experiences, this book would not have been possible. Thanks to all of you.

Before Reading This Book

The book you are about to read is a true story about team effort and leadership accomplished in excellence in the midst of a national crisis. As you read, the first anomaly you will notice is the use of job position identifiers rather than personal names. I would like to have named all the people who did so many things both the right way and for the right reasons throughout the space shuttle Columbia disaster and response, but I would surely have missed someone. Additionally, I have left out the majority of faux pas and foul ups that invariably happen in any high-pressure situation. Be assured not everything proceeded according to plan. We tried to learn from each stumble, however, encourage each other, and move on. Except for chapter four, I have used only mild issues for examples where appropriate.

Several people have asked me, "Why write another book on leadership? And why write one about leadership in times of crisis?" My answer is simple: because it is needed. Disaster and large-scale incidents are growing in size, scope, and intensity on the American landscape.

With this growth comes the commensurate need for good leadership during those times, and leaders who function in a normal daily environment do not necessarily make the best crisis leaders. Pressure, time, and intensity freeze some leaders while it frees others.

America is not totally lacking in preparation for disasters, but I have not observed a balanced approach.

- Federal, state, and local governments are attempting to prepare at some level for future disasters, but there are at least two challenges. First, funds are limited for needed equipment; second, training of rescue skills that can become weak when not used regularly must be refreshed on a regular basis. That takes additional money. Being ready at all times for any disaster or crisis boils down to equipment, time, and money, the things we all seem to be short of.

- While a great deal of work is ongoing in teaching elements of the National Response Plan, including inculcating the National Incident Management System throughout all levels of the emergency response world, these preparations are not adequately dealing with person to person leadership principles and skills. We are building a sturdy functional framework but may soon find ourselves lacking the people skills needed to make the framework work smoothly under the pressures of crisis.

- Leadership is not management, yet more and more books and seminars are parading management across the landscape with the word "leadership" as a façade. The two words both indicate necessary skill sets but are not synonymous, and therefore leaders in all levels of public, corporate, and private business would do well to keep the two separate but equal in their efforts to improve.

Finally, be assured that this book is not intended in any way to be a comprehensive book on leadership during crisis, but only a starting point. As you read, I hope you will both enjoy the story and glean useful leadership principles. The greater desire I have, though, is that you will read the lessons learned with the foremost questions being, what can I learn from this, and what do I need to do to implement the fundamentals of crisis leadership when I need them most – facing the next crisis?

CHAPTER 1

AND THE SKY FELL

A deep, thick rumble resounded in the air early Saturday morning, February 1, 2003, wakening the habitants of East Texas to what would be a monumental day in present history. Like a train derailing, the roar of a spring storm, or even the implosion of a large building in the distance, the rumble lasted only for scant moments before fading into an eerie silence. Almost everyone, except experts at the NASA Space Center in Houston, was left completely unaware.

At 8:00 a.m. that harrowing Saturday morning, STS-107 entered the Earth's atmosphere and quickly disintegrated while en route to what should have been a routine re-entry for landing in Florida. Better known as Space Shuttle Columbia, the vessel had been orbiting the Earth for almost 16 days on a multidisciplinary microgravity and Earth science research mission. On board the shuttle were Commander Rick D. Husband,

1

Pilot William C. McCool, Mission Specialists David M. Brown, Laurel B. Clark, and Kalpana Chawla, Payload Commander Michael P. Anderson, and Ilan Ramon, a payload specialist from the Israeli Air Force. The mission was a statistical success in terms of research gathered, though sadly each astronaut would finish the course of their lives in the skies over East Texas that morning.

Traveling near speeds of Mach 10, the shuttle entry literally began to fall apart as it entered air space over the United States West Coast, shedding its first piece of debris somewhere over California. But the vast majority of the craft was to eventually land in Texas, primarily East Texas. In a matter of minutes, the shuttle Columbia had been reduced to fragments scattered over more than 2,000 different debris fields. Reports flooded emergency lines across Texas, southwestern Arkansas, and parts of Louisiana; NASA locked its doors and hunkered down for the long haul. The sky had fallen.

The sky can fall for anyone in leadership at anytime. We just never know when that time might be. One challenge is that a disaster to one leader is a mere inconvenience to another. Regardless of the circumstances, however, ultimate success in dealing with nearly any disaster is dependent on the '4 P' rule – people, planning, practice, and past experience. Nacogdoches County was no different on that early Saturday morning of February 1, 2003. It took willing people, working with a flexible and well practiced plan, and using lessons learned from past experiences to accomplish the herculean tasks that began on that day.

Nacogdoches County is a very rural community. Poultry production, timber raising, logging, and small businesses make up the majority of the economy that supports the people within the community. Emergency services are a collection of paid professionals and willing and hard-working volunteers. The county seat, the city of Nacogdoches, bills itself as the "Oldest Town in Texas," and some would argue that entrenched ideas and leadership styles are consistent with this marketed perception. That all changed when the sky fell.

In just minutes, Nacogdoches became the epicenter of the shuttle debris trail and the focus of attention for recovery efforts. For the next fourteen days, Nacogdoches would prove that leadership during times of disaster can be focused, effective, and professional. During those fourteen days, the leadership team would deal with people who responded from over 120 agencies from around the world, deal with news media on a daily basis, and coordinate with NASA and other government agencies in operating an effective recovery operation. They would learn first-hand what leadership principles work in the pressure of disaster situations, and those that are useless ideas with no practical application. The rest of this book is dedicated to sharing the good, the bad, and the sometimes ugly of leadership lessons learned when the sky fell.

To best understand any lessons learned, one must first have an understanding of the disciplines, perceptions, and expectations of the people who responded to the Columbia tragedy. First of all, Texas state law prescribes that during any officially declared emergency the county judge, the highest elected official in a county, is the Emergency Director. The county judge can delegate much of the responsibility to another individual known as the Emergency Management Coordinator or Director of Homeland Security for that county. But the final decision and responsibility rests with the Emergency Director.

Secondly, in line with directions from the National Response Plan, a part of the disaster preparedness planning for the entire United States, Nacogdoches officials had learned and based response control on the Incident Command System, known simply as ICS. An oversimplified definition of ICS is that it is a flexible, codified method of managing response, personnel, and resources for any disaster, regardless of size. ICS has been in use for decades in the United States, and has even made the cross-over into the corporate world using various names and nomenclatures.

Utilizing ICS, there is a designated Incident Commander, followed by leaders in four designated broad discipline areas, with each broad area further broken into smaller parts as appropriate. If a disaster is extremely large in scope, either in geographic or cataclysmic nature, there can also be a Unified Command structure added above the ICS structure. The Unified Command, or UC, is intended to be the coordination point for multiple ICS command structures that may be scattered out over a large geographic area. Because of the way Unified Command is currently defined, it poses significant challenges in the way disasters are handled, and can be an example to leaders in every discipline of the way things should not be handled.

The beauty of the ICS system, however, is that it is flexible and is intended to follow the natural flow of responder disciplines, needs, and issues. There is a single acknowledged leader. ICS can start with just two people, an Incident Commander (IC) and a responder, and grow to thousands without creating chaos or losing command and control of a situation. In Nacogdoches, ICS was immediately implemented when the scope of the disaster was understood. I became the designated Incident Commander for those first days, and was responsible for overall coordination of the response efforts within our county. Leadership during the disaster was not about "me," as it should never be with any leader, but rather about our team of leaders who understood their strengths, talents, and focus, and empowered those around them to simply do their job well.

The lessons learned were many, and those are shared within the following pages. Beginning the second day, I began recording thoughts, lessons, and challenges at the end of every day based around four basic questions.

1. What went right today? A leader should always identify victories within an organization in order to encourage and reinforce good habits and continued positive growth.

2. What was a challenge today? Rather than saying "what went wrong," leaders should consider issues and concerns that do not end up well as challenges to overcome. People generally know when something goes wrong in a crisis. They neither need reinforcement of the "wrong," nor do they appreciate it. Rather, by considering a 'challenge,' hope is given that there can be, and truly is, an

answer within their control. They just need to find it.

3. What future issues and concerns can I anticipate surrounding this crisis in the next 12, 24, 48, and 72 hours? In times of crisis, it is of paramount importance that leaders think "ahead of the curve" in specific time increments. Questions with timelines help focus what is truly important for immediate future versus what may not have strong impact until a later time. In this manner, both resources and energy are directed and focused properly.

4. In light of answers to the first two questions, what are the options for dealing with the issues identified in question number three? This particular question is where I began to connect the dots and make effective plans, as it brought forth so many other necessary questions that were anticipatory in nature. What physical resources might we need? What agencies needed to be involved? Who were the key influencers needed to bring success? At this point, there were literally dozens of questions that I asked myself.

Before you continue further in this book, I must enumerate a few key points in order to give a solid base of future reference. The first key point is about leadership in general. It has been fascinating to see the focus placed on the term "leadership" in the past few years, yet alarming to see the diversity with which it has been defined. A simple word has been expanded to be either a cover excuse for pure management styles, or a complicated academic term that is difficult to apply. Let me keep it simple – ***leadership is influence***. No, the concept is not of my own origination, but it is the key to understanding effective leadership in times of crisis.

Secondly, crises bring out the best and worst in both people and organizations. Honest team critique is crucial to learning for the future, while singling individuals out for criticism has no benefit and should never be a part of a leader's tool box. With this in mind, I will strive to share corporate mistakes and lessons learned, while leaving individual names out. Additionally, I will be transparent where appropriate about my own foibles and failings, as a good leader will never try to position himself/herself as the "be all – end all." True leaders have a continual learning mentality, and there is no more effective classroom than a crisis or disaster. As you read on, put yourself in your last crisis, and ask yourself, "What would I do differently now?"

Finally, you will encounter a series of Crisis Leadership Lessons (CLL) as you go through the book. As a leader, few should surprise you in their simplicity, but you will be challenged to see if you can apply them during disasters. I challenge you to think about each one in the context of our disaster and ask yourself, "Do I really do this during my own crises or disasters?" Your honest answer may surprise you.

Onward now. The sky has fallen. The pieces are still floating to earth. And it is time to throw out the book of what we think we know.

CHAPTER 2

THROW OUT THE BOOK

"Well, how do we want to handle this, Bob?" This question greeted me as I entered the Nacogdoches Sheriff's Office dispatch area. The Lieutenant on duty as Watch Commander was an extremely experienced and competent officer and had quickly grasped the fact that this event was unlike any disaster we had ever encountered. Tornadoes, floods, wildfires, HAZMATs and even the occasional hurricane were events we had both faced over the years. This was different.

What do you do when the unbelievable happens – a space craft falls apart over your head? I quickly realized what I would later call Crisis Leadership Lesson #1; we had to quickly define the scope of the incident in order to make a swift and orderly response. In spite of all the response guidelines and "rule books" the Lieutenant and I had read, not one of them had a chapter called, "Space Shuttle Disintegration on Orbital Reentry." Without known guidelines, I did the only thing left to do: I quickly ran through my memory of any experience similar to this one from which I could possibly draw an appropriate response. In this case, that meant a plane crash.

"Immediately instruct your officers responding to debris calls to note the location, document the person who reported it and guard the piece of debris. Let's attempt to preserve pieces as though they are evidence from an airplane crash. Photograph them for pictorial documentation, at least until we get further direction," I said.

> **CLL -** The leader should initially define the scope of the disaster as quickly as reasonable. This offers guidance on structure, needs, and provides a "handle" for the leader to hold on to.

With this simple agreement between us, response efforts began. As of yet, we had not begun to grasp the true scope of the disaster, yet still we were able to begin the process of placing parameters in order to provide a working definition for the responders. Like King David of the Bible, we were facing a monstrous Goliath that demanded an answer; and like David, we soon found it necessary to dispense with conventional means so as to conquer this monumental challenge. We had ample reason for an unconventional response to this situation.

Debris strike reports kept flooding in as we further developed our initial response actions in those first few minutes. Hundreds of questions raced through my mind forcing me to anticipate various scenarios. *Was anyone in our county hurt by falling debris? What about people in the unincorporated county areas —what is the best way to quickly canvas the areas and verify that no one is lying somewhere injured and needing assistance? What is the status of the astronauts aboard? If they have perished, will we potentially find their remains? What if civilians find human remains? How will they handle it? Was there hazardous cargo on board, such as bio-hazardous medical experiments, fuel cells, or even nuclear materials in some type of low-level reactor? How many pieces might there be and how will we secure them all? Were there any TOP SECRET materials we needed to be aware of, and how do authorities want us to handle those? Where will the additional manpower needed to guard and/or recover debris come from? How quickly can we get our off-duty personnel recalled to duty? What is the status of NASA and other federal agencies? When will they arrive, and where will we stage their operations? What about the press? If this is as big an incident as suspected, there will inevitably be a large number of press corps. Where will we have them park their satellite vans that will allow them to do their job, yet keep them out of our way? How quickly can we get our leadership team together to begin handling our response?*

On and on and on the questions swirled through my mind, and with each question

CLL - When necessary, be unafraid to "throw out the book" of structured planning and adapt quickly to a resilient, flexible style of leadership. In a dynamic and fluid situation, your formal plan becomes a guiding light rather than a fixated anchor.

came multiple answers. Each potential answer prompted a clearer possible plan of action, and each answer illuminated the precarious truth that this was unlike any disaster for which we had planned or practiced. We had to "throw out the book" of the past and adapt quickly to the present needs.

At this point, agencies and emergency personnel throughout our county were beginning to contact us with their own reports and questions. Though we had no solid answers, we utilized each call to engage the party or agency in our general plans for immediate response. I was extremely thankful now for the time taken in the past to develop personal and agency relationships prior to the disaster; because of built-in trust, people were willing to follow our dynamic and fluid plan of action for the moment. We had neither the time nor freedom for extensive discussion and planning, therefore what allowed us to influence directions at a critical time was the foundation of developed relationships.

> **CLL** – Crisis leadership is the influence developed through prior relationships, and now compressed by time and present circumstances. Develop good working relationships BEFORE a crisis or disaster occurs.

Adding to the pressure of time compression was the issue of divergent differences in equipment, training, and capabilities across our county. Like any predominantly rural county, Nacogdoches County consists of volunteer emergency workers of various disciplines and training levels who often work emergencies side by side with full-time career emergency personnel. The disaster began to grow exponentially, quickly outstripping our pool of personnel and available resources. An officer with the local Texas National Guard contacted our Emergency Operations Center (EOC) and offered his personnel to assist us. The Guard happened to be in the midst of a scheduled weekend drill. We immediately accepted their offer and quickly placed all personnel in the field.

As time progressed in the early stages of the response, a new issue began to rapidly inject itself into the scheme of leadership concerns, and this issue was one for which leaders must always be prepared. In times of crisis, a persons' perception is working reality for the moment. This perception may or may not be factual, but it will inevitably comprise the working mental framework for that person during that moment in time.

Take this perceptual reality truth and expand it across many agencies, crossing multiple technical and logistical disciplines. The result is a cauldron of emotions and expectations that possess the potential for a strong negative impact on the situation. When faced with a large disaster or crisis, the leader must anticipate this perception issue and be prepared to communicate goals and expectations clearly for the entire organization. People

> **CLL** – Perception is reality, but it may not be factual. Anticipate flawed perceptions and be prepared to swiftly counter them with clearly communicated goals and expectations.

subconsciously crave the assurance that **someone** is in charge of the chaos!

Perception differences had huge implications for our operations and shuttle recovery. For NASA, Columbia was their space craft and the astronauts were their friends, family and professional colleagues. Their professional perception of the crisis was rife with the complexity of emotional and technical attachment and responsibility. They filtered thousands of their own questions and issues through internal channels beneath the weighty pressure of a watching world. *What went wrong? Why? How do we ever determine with finality what happened when the debris is scattered across such a wide span of terrain? Did our friends suffer? What do we tell the astronauts' families? What happens now?*

Federal law enforcement agencies also had specific concerns. *Was this a terrorist incident? If so, how did they do it? Do we have a major security breach that contributed to the demise of the shuttle? If not terrorism, then what caused this? Were there TOP SECRET materials aboard? Were they destroyed? What was the purpose of the materials, and is there a risk to national security? Were there scientific instruments aboard that are considered TOP SECRET? Did they burn up, or are they lying in a field waiting to be discovered?* Just imagine the unease, almost panic, these federal law officers must have felt, and how desperate they were to quickly find answers.

In the first ninety minutes of the unfolding disaster, I received phone calls at our EOC from the Federal Bureau of Investigation, Federal Marshalls Service, U.S. Secret Service, the Alcohol, Tobacco and Firearms Administration, and three other federal agencies. Each agency had its own perspectives of the developing disaster, its own questions and concerns, and each insisted a different plan of action be taken.

State authorities approached the disaster from yet another viewpoint. This incident was unfolding across a multi-county area of Texas, a state that has always taken pride in its "can do" attitude. In the midst of the confusion, Texas emergency officials knew the world would be watching Texas' efforts in acting as the intermediary between local concerns and responses, and federal directions and needs.

Overall, every agency was suddenly faced with a unique disaster that followed no clear cut guidelines from past experience. The result was a need to rapidly take any planned response plan and resize it. Be aware that you, too, may have to one day do the same if the sky begins to fall around you.

CHAPTER 3

RESIZE IT!

"Let me introduce myself. I'm the Fire Chief at the Dallas-Ft. Worth International Airport, and we're here to help in any way we can. I know you didn't call us, but we headed this way when the disaster occurred and heard how Nacogdoches seems to be in the center of this disaster, so we came here. I have a mobile command post out front, a complete crew to man it, and all we want to know is how can we assist you?" Thus began my introduction into the world of large scale disasters. Out of nowhere, an agency from outside our area had appeared with an asset that would soon prove invaluable to the expanding size of the operation. This was one of *many* similar offers of personnel and equipment we would encounter over the coming days and weeks, and each needed to be addressed in a cogent fashion. We had to resize everything, our scope, our resources, but most of all, our mindset. It became apparent very quickly that if we were to responsibly handle the myriad of people and resources that were headed our general direction, we had to have some type of structure in place.

When a disaster or crisis seems overwhelming to the leader(s) or leadership team, rapid resizing must take place quickly on two fronts. First, the organizational response structure must be adjusted; second, and less definable but even more critical, the essence of leadership must also undergo adjustment. The first issue, the organization response structure, is well-defined and time-tested in the Incident Command System (ICS). If you are unfamiliar with ICS, it starts with the first person to respond to the incident, crisis, or disaster. It can then dynamically grow and shrink, according to the needs of the situation, to thousands of people or just the original two. As it grows, ICS defines four major functional areas of focus: operations, logistics, planning, and finance. The entire ICS team is led by a single person designated the Incident Commander (IC.) Within each of these four silos of activity in the public response arena there can be, and usually is, further definition of functionality, i.e. fire fighting, law enforcement, rescue, lodging, responder rehab, planning for the future, tracking specific expenses, etc. ICS is designed to bring "order to the chaos" by giving organizational structure, which it does well. ICS is so ingrained in the emergency response community that it has now become a part of the National Response Plan for the United States.

> **CLL-** Be prepared to resize everything in times of disaster, including your leadership mindset!

Companies and organizations would do well to study and learn how to practically implement ICS within their leadership structure. (More information can be found online at http://www.fema.gov/emergency/nims/ .)

Though ICS is certainly a proven method when building dynamic disaster and crisis management teams, it does not effectively address several major leadership issues that must also expand. Through the experience of the shuttle Columbia tragedy, I have noted that leadership issues are generally more difficult to define. During the early hours of the shuttle disaster response, for instance, the challenge for our leadership team surfaced when balancing needs, expectations, capabilities, desires, training, and experience with the present and anticipated needs in the field of operation. Our entire leadership team had to rapidly evaluate response assets and ascertain whether people were being placed into a dynamically fluid situation such that their efforts worked in concert and not against each other. That last sentence is a fancy way of saying we had to be certain the right people were in the right position doing the right job to get the best results!

Our entire leadership team was quickly confronted with the fact that the key to success was going to be flexibility- both personally and professionally. In the midst of the semi-rigid framework of ICS, we

> **CLL** – Key word in disaster leadership – *FLEXIBILITY!* Flexibility in your command and leadership structure allows you to see the changes in the "big picture" of the crisis more quickly.

first had to determine skill needs for the operations, incident scope size, and where these needs fit within the skill sets of the people immediately available. We discovered, however, that a big key in crisis is to surround yourself with identified team members who are not only capable and willing to help, but can also do so *in a positive manner*. This means that some people with positional authority (they have a higher rank within an organization) may find it necessary to be flexible and cede actions and leadership decisions to others in the overall operation without grumbling or undermining the leadership team. A positive example of this professionalism and flexibility occurred early in our response operations.

Near the middle of the afternoon on the first day of response (Saturday, Feb. 1st), the DFW fire chief approached me in the Command Post (CP) with a specific, well defined challenge his crew was facing in handling incoming calls for debris and/or assistance. Though he had a professional background that would have normally prompted him to make a decision and move on, he was also cognizant that his crew was there to assist us. Therefore, after stating the challenge, along with several possible resolutions, he closed by saying to me, "There it is (*the problem and resolution options*), and I need a command decision NOW." In spite of his positional authority and depth of previous experience, he knew he had to be professionally flexible and seek my input as the local Incident Commander (IC.) Hold that train of thought for a moment, and allow me to address another issue that leaders must face in crisis leadership when dealing with people and a rapidly expanding crisis.

I have observed over the years that there is a scarcity of leaders who will ask a very key question prior to making impactful decisions. *"What are the unintended consequences of this decision?"* It is a simple question, but

CLL – In times of crisis or disaster, the leader must understand his/her scope of responsibility and actions they can and should take and communicate that scope quickly and clearly.

addressing it can save much time, confusion, and energy. It is a question that in itself is flexible, needing only scant seconds of thought, maybe a few pertinent questions for additional information, and maybe a group discussion for input if time warrants. However it is addressed, the question is an absolute necessity when leading in crises or disasters. Our leadership team continually framed answers to issues and problems with this question. There were several times that we redirected our answer because of potentially negative issues identified through this process of questioning. With the fire chief now standing before me, I applied the process of questioning unintended consequences, and after an additional question or two, the chief returned to his crew with a new operational direction.

In the example above, there is yet another leadership point that is worthy of further clarification. In times of crisis, the leader must understand his or her scope of responsibility and actions he/she can and should take; he/she must then communicate that scope quickly and clearly to those working with the crisis. For instance, as

IC I had certain functional expectations and requirements within ICS to fulfill. However, I made it clear to all team members that there were also several responsibilities that I was incorporating into both my position and into the entire leadership team at the time. The following enumerated items are taken from old briefing notes that I employed as a guide during the actual team meetings. I repeated these five items at the end of every meeting for the first week of operations, and later had abundant feedback from professionals in all disciplines that these points helped keep a clear perspective on the structure of the operations.

1. It is my (the Incident Commander) responsibility to make certain that you (the various responding agencies) have all the tools and equipment you feel you need to do your job safely and completely. If you cannot get it, come to me, and I will make certain you get it.

2. It is my responsibility to make certain that you are not hindered in doing your job. If you have a situation that you cannot resolve through your channels, bring it to me and we will get it resolved.

3. It is my responsibility to "take the bullet" for you if necessary. If a situation arises that creates any kind of challenge for you that you cannot handle in the field, bring it to me and we will get it resolved.

4. After stating these first three points, let me make something crystal clear. It is NOT my job to do your job, to tell you how to do your job, or to try to influence you to do your job a certain way unless safety is involved. We *(our leadership team)* have set clear goals for this operation, and we ask you to run your operation with those goals foremost in your mind. Other than that, you are professionals, you know your job, and we know you will do your job well.

5. Finally, let me remind you of a critical point. It has been my observation that anything in nature that has more than one head is considered a freak. The same is true in leadership, particularly in times of crisis. There is one IC and that is me. I am responsible to our County Judge. Our state law says she is the final boss in disasters in this county but that she can also delegate certain portions of that authority. With her consent and direction, I am the IC. That fact does not negate any of the other points I have stated, but it does mean two things: First, no surprises, please. Make certain you are bringing full information disclosure to these meetings so that all team members are kept in the information loop. Second, if a decision has to be brought to this level, the final decision will rest here (IC) and not in a committee. Therefore, we encourage you to do everything you can to

> collaborate with each other to create win-win
> answers on any issues that arise in the field.

Thankfully, we were able to identify and quickly surround our operations with cooperative and clearly focused people on that first day. The DFW Fire Chief brought his mobile command unit and a team of trained professionals to man it. We rapidly shifted the answering of the massive number of incoming debris report calls to their team, relieving an intense burden from our Sheriff's Office operators. The Texas National Guard personnel were quickly dispatched into the field to assist in standing guard over pieces of debris. Our local Volunteer Fire Departments did yeoman service in conducting initial searches throughout their individual fire districts, seeking people who might have been injured by falling debris. They also watched for homes and buildings that might have been damaged. Everyone was professional and positive in his or her actions, which in turn kept the leadership team focused on the other issues of "resizing."

Another discipline that leaders must address in resizing disaster and crisis response is actively working to anticipate important issues. The key word is "anticipate." Early in our disaster operations, I set a discipline within my personal expectations framework of occasionally repeating to myself, "One, four, twelve, three." When I did this, I was taking the time to think in specific time increments about the anticipated physical, logistical, and psychological needs of the operations. What might be needed in the next hour that we did not already have in motion? What about the next four hours? Was there specialized equipment, personnel, or other resources we needed to be ordering now so that we could have it when needed? In twelve hours, personnel would be reaching the end of their physical limits; were we ready to accommodate their needs for

CLL – In a crisis, leaders must anticipate in specific time increments.

rest and nourishment? What resources would be nearing depletion at the end of three days? Did we need to replace that resource, or could we let it go? If we needed to replenish or replace, did we need to be ordering it now to have it then?

As I ran through each question, I always framed my point of reference around three words: protect, perspective, proceed. Protect stood for safety. Were we still conducting safe operations? Were we taking all measures necessary to protect our team members physically, emotionally, and mentally? Perspective reminded me to occasionally stop and look at the entire operation from a different angle. Was there any need, issue or leadership point that was so obvious I was missing it? Was I "so close to the trees that I was missing the forest?" At one point, just to make certain I was not running in a "thought rut" as the IC, I climbed up on a table and watched the briefing room as people filed in for one of the team leader meetings. Things look different from only three feet off the floor, and the activity was a good reminder that I needed to do the same

CLL – "Three P's" of crisis leadership.
Protect,
Perspective,
Proceed.

table climbing mentally. Only after I assured myself that "protect" was completed, and that my "perspective" had truly taken in all possible contingencies did I move on to "proceed" and worked to plan and execute an updated plan with the leadership team.

One word of caution here as we discuss resizing, or scaling up, operations in disasters: It is absolutely imperative that the key leader(s) set the operational tempo for the entire team *early* in the operation. If you are the key leader, your <u>attitude</u> will have a direct effect on your entire teams' <u>aptitude</u> to function effectively. What do I mean by this? Unfortunately, I have life examples to offer.

Leader 'A' is a dynamic individual who has positional authority within an organization, company, or group. Accustomed to being in control, Leader 'A' expects people to respond immediately when called on a daily basis. This leader makes it clear that he/she is the answer to the needs of the team or organization, whatever those "needs" are. Leader 'B' is also a dynamic individual with positional authority in the company or organization. Leader 'B,' however, understands that people are the richest asset of the organization and constantly works to build a spirit of teamwork where team members are both encouraged to strive for excellence and also seek to make life a series of win-win situations; everyone wins.

Along comes a disaster or crisis, and Leader 'A' now goes into command and control mode as that is how he/she is most comfortable leading on a daily basis. Forceful commands, yelling, and extreme angst quickly become tools for exacting actions based on demands by this leader; the result is a team that cowers, clams up, and functions sub-optimally. Leader 'A' has just set an operational tempo that will cause the team to function at far below its potential.

Leader 'B,' on the other hand, handles the high energy produced by the crisis differently. He/she works immediately to 'protect, get perspective, and proceed.' Is everyone safe? What is the big picture and scope of what has occurred, and what are the impacts? What plan will most swiftly lead to as successful a resolution as possible; what can we do to build a win-win? Leader 'B' has just faced the same challenge as Leader 'A' but has set a much different operational tempo for the response. "I'm in charge" has been replaced with "We are a team. We can do this together." "My way or the high way" has been replaced with, "Who has the best idea, and how quickly can we as a team implement it?" Trust me when I say that Leader 'B's' team is going to be the one to bring the disaster or crisis to a more successful resolution. Setting the operational tempo early and often is critical for leader(s) during times of organizational crisis.

> **CLL – *Set the operational tempo early.*** The leader's ATTITUDE will directly affect the teams' response APTITUDE, or effectiveness.

What happens when something so big and so overwhelming occurs that the leader(s) realizes it cannot be handled with his/her current capabilities? Simple: Ask for help. When help arrives, do not let resources, whether people or equipment, leave until you are absolutely certain the resource will not be needed; otherwise, you may miss a gem of an opportunity. Here is another example.

Several days into the shuttle recovery operations, a process had been defined for handling recovered debris in Nacogdoches County. When found, the debris part was first rendered safe, if needed, and then a GPS fix (Global Positioning System) was determined prior to being removed to a central collection point. At the central collection point for our county, the Nacogdoches County Exposition Center, the debris was then logged in, tagged, and set aside for a NASA vehicle and crew to load at the end of the day. The NASA personnel would then take the tagged debris to Barksdale Air Force Base in Shreveport, Louisiana for final airlift to Cape Canaveral, Florida.

One afternoon, an older gentleman approached the team at the Exposition Center debris collection point and asked if he could assist in any manner. Politely, he was told that his offer was appreciated but his services were not needed. At this point, we had more volunteers in our county than we ever imagined would arrive. The gentleman persisted and asked to be allowed to assist in the debris tagging and log-in. As the story is recounted, the team leader was in the process of trying to politely send the man away when the man suddenly said, "You don't understand, I helped build this ship. I know where the parts fit!" Somewhat startled, the team leader wisely asked for more information.

The man recounted how he had worked for years with NASA in the shuttle program. Eventually, he became one of the lead engineers on the shuttle Columbia construction project and was in a supervisory position as the shuttle transformed from the drawing board to a completed space craft ready to take its maiden voyage.

> **CLL –** Be careful not to overlook useful resources right in your "backyard" of operations. Be open-minded, listen and observe.

When he said he knew where the parts were supposed to go, he meant it...literally! Upon retirement from NASA, he had moved to a small town in the north end of our county and was now presenting himself as a willing and knowledgeable worker. His understanding proved to be of immeasurable value to the debris tagging operations. And just think, we nearly let this resource leave because we did not realize how 'big' his knowledge of the issue was; it was "shuttle size." Now that is sizing it up! Always be prepared, if you find yourself in a leadership position in a crisis or disaster, to resize it, even to "shuttle size" if necessary!

CHAPTER 4

Bumps, Potholes, and Detours

In the days that followed the initial descent of the shuttle, debris reports flooded our systems; agencies from across the United States entered and exited our command center and the enormity of our responsibilities began to weigh in on us. The majority of the time, we would be rapidly speeding along in our recovery operations. However, I noticed that occasionally we would hit a few small bumps, some major potholes, and take a detour every once in a while. Slowly, it dawned on me that what was occurring was typical because we are human; but for our progress's sake, these issues had to be dealt with promptly and directly. Let me recount a more dramatic example of this.

On day four of the operation, one of the men in the Nacogdoches leadership team entered the EOC visibly upset. The people under his direction, highly trained geospatial information systems (GIS) technicians, had been responsible for gathering information on all shuttle pieces and remains, and storing that information for later use. As a result, his technicians had gathered highly sensitive information throughout the recovery operation and had set commensurate electronic safeguards in place to protect the data. The previous day, however, representatives from another governmental organization within the recovery operation had contacted his men and threatened to physically take the GIS computers and reformat the hard drives in the field, even though sufficient safeguards had been set in place. Their methods of deleting the information would wipe out any other important data gathered and stored on the computer, whether or not it was related to the recovery operations. Both the means and the methods were unacceptable, but the motivation behind it was well-intentioned. The information being gathered was not life-threatening or life-saving; it was, however, sensitive.

I quickly contacted my liaison with the agency and after a few phone calls, the situation was alleviated and the relationship restored. The breakdown, however, was obvious: this agency had taken notice of an important effort and then become fixated on it to the point of slowing the progress of other organizations.

"Fixation" for crisis leadership is exactly what the word means: a preoccupation or obsession with one subject or thing. Fixation can be a major issue for leaders during any time or type of crisis. Fixation is both divisive and detrimental to progress. It's like pouring thick syrup in the gears of progress; everything slows down and tends to get very sticky.

Fixation occurs on all levels and is caused by a number of things. Usually, it occurs because someone becomes intent on solving a problem or situation; the problem is often something that pertains to his/her specialty or background in training. Nonetheless, the problem with fixation is that it causes one to lose sight of the big picture, to major on the minor. Personality, experience, and background impacts one's perspective, and a person's perspective motivates his or her pressure points, or points of fixation. Furthermore, when a person does not feel that what he/she believes is important or valued by the others around him/her, it causes that person to fixate even more on the issue. Therefore, it's important to listen to and validate the opinions of others whether or not you act upon their suggestions.

In crisis leadership, it is important to deal with fixation directly and swiftly lest you lose too much time. Remember, though, that

> **CLL -** Beware of fixation on a single issue, person or event within the crisis or disaster, whether within yourself, or within your team.

emotions are high in disasters and the leader must be able to be direct while keeping a calm demeanor. The best way to deal with fixation is to pre-empt it. Expect that some fixation will occur, so combat it by setting standards in place that will help minimize it as much as possible. Our intended way of dealing with fixation internally was to encourage and ensure that each and every person working the recovery was filtering all concerns and questions through the goals we had previously decided upon (detailed in chapter 2). The filtering process not only helped to cull through the less urgent items, it also helped flag the issues that *were* important and worthy of immediate action.

Remember that people will tend to become fixated more quickly when they are distraught or involved emotionally in the crisis or disaster at hand. This certainly could have been the case for the NASA astronaut corps during the shuttle disaster. Instead, it was both fascinating and humbling to observe the responses of the NASA personnel with whom I had the privilege of working.

Barely three hours after the crash occurred, two astronauts entered the Nacogdoches command center. They had heard that we had possibly recovered some bodies of the astronauts killed in the tragedy at hand. After initial introductions, in my ignorance, I asked them how well they knew the astronauts aboard. Their response: "They are our family. We've come to take them home." Until this point in time, the tragedy was solely intellectual; now it was personal. As I informed them that the information was in error, I suddenly realized that the astronauts that train with NASA are not only colleagues, they are family; NASA had lost seven of its family members. They could have crumbled under the effects of such devastating news. Instead, they were the vanguard of professionalism in their directing and facilitating, never allowing themselves to be visibly affected by the loss until all work was done. There would be time to grieve later, but for now they did not allow themselves to suffer fixation but were consummate professionals in assistance, poise, and demeanor. Not only did their composure help them work efficiently in the recovery efforts, it was contagious and set an example for others aiding them in their decision-making.

Another important pothole for crisis leadership is very similar to fixation, but with a different scope: distraction. Whereas fixation is normally born of previous experience, background, and expertise, distraction can happen to anyone. Distractions lure people away from the main goals and lead them down long detours of slow progress, or no progress at all. Distractions allow the

> **CLL -** Distractions – the tyranny of the urgent overrunning what is truly important. The leaders' key phrase? **"Control your focus!"**

tyranny of the urgent to rule process and decision-making instead of keeping the big picture in mind. In the end, distractions rob you of time, energy, and clarity of thought.

During crises or disasters, you can count on distractions developing. By nature, crises and disasters are jam-packed with emotionally charged occurrences and the most distracting things are loaded with emotion. Compound this issue with a lack of down-time for personnel and you have a perfect recipe for distraction. People are more likely to have their attention diverted when they are tired and cannot focus properly.

Fortunately for us during the shuttle recovery operations, our command center shut down for at least a few hours every evening, forcing people to rest. In long-running disasters, however, it is normal for leaders to let rest be a peripheral issue. In fact, in most disaster operations, leadership often loses track of who has been resting and who has not. The result can be a team of people who begin to make poor decisions because of fatigue. As a leader, it is important to keep track of this not just for your people, but more importantly for yourself. I almost learned the hard way.

When the disaster recovery operations began, I would arrive at the EOC around 5:30 in the morning and would not leave sometimes until after midnight. At the end of each day, we would debrief and plan for the next day. I would arrive early the next morning to get things set up for our first personnel briefing of the day. We were all busy; we were all focused; we were all wearing down.

One of the men in our leadership team, a man who had worked the disaster operations of large-scale forest fires for years finally approached me at one point and very directly told me to quit trying to be at the command center all the time. "Slow down; stop. Get some rest. You're going to burn yourself out. Besides that, as the Incident Commander, you are not setting a good example of balance for the others in the team." At first, being the type A personality that I am, I was a bit irritated; I wanted to be in the middle of everything all the time. But I respected this man's knowledge and years of experience, so I began to think about a change of pace. One night, I came home and my daughter said to me, "You know dad, I've never seen you this energized and focused, but you look awful right now!", It was true, I was energized because I was living out my years of training and passion, but I looked awful because I was not getting enough rest. Distraction was taking my focus from the larger picture of the operations. Lack of adequate rest is just one example of what distraction can do.

Distraction will happen, so it is better to expect and prepare for it so as to deal with it properly. Leaders must be intentional about not focusing on the distractions but instead asking the most efficient questions when new information comes across his or her desk. The next chapter is devoted specifically to good communication during disasters, including asking the right questions.

If fixation and distractions are irritating issues for crisis leadership, then information overload is possibly the most devastating of potholes to fall in. Information overload can shut down the senses, both physical and mental. For us, the information overload issue started immediately. For example, when the shuttle collapsed over Nacogdoches, our 9-1-1 dispatch system was so jammed with phone calls from all over the county that for over six hours the system could not electronically timestamp the calls on the recording system, as is customary for all 9-1-1 systems. The dispatchers never put their phone receivers down; they just punched a new lighted button for the next call. The amount of incoming information was overwhelming, and we had to quickly get some type of control in place. Eventually, after the DFW Airport Mobile Command bus arrived and set up, the dispatchers

> **CLL -** Information overload will lead the entire leadership team down detours that dead end. Leadership must build processes to sift the important information from the superfluous quickly.

began to transfer all shuttle debris related phone calls to operators in the mobile command center, thereby alleviating some of the overload on our system. This issue of information overload is another reason that we quickly delineated our top three goals. This way, everyone had a set of very specific questions through which to filter the overflow of incoming information. Goal 1: Is it a safety issue? Goal 2: Will it help NASA more quickly recover the shuttle? Goal 3: Would it help our county return to normal? Goals can be of great assistance in guiding around the potholes in disasters.

Additionally, when information is being received with such rapidity and in such large quantities, it is vital that leaders know where their resources are. At one point, we received a call from a local farmer who swore that fallout from the shuttle was killing his deer. Fortunately, we had a man on our leadership team who was also a nationally recognized deer expert. He addressed the issue, determined that the deaths were natural and not debris related, and the newest "crisis" was over almost as quickly as it had begun. When in a position of leadership during a crisis or disaster, know your resources and be ready to call on them as soon as the need arises. Delegate parts of the information overload to those that can handle it. Do not wait until the situation is out of hand. Our leadership team never did, and it paid dividends in efficiency.

Another common downfall for leaders is trying to play the hero and handle everything themselves, rather than relying on more knowledgeable or prepared resources. A key phrase for leaders in times of complete uncertainty is: "I don't know," followed quickly by, "Let's find someone who does." There is no way that one person will have all

> CLL - Know who your knowledge resources are, or find them quickly. Don't even try to act like you know every answer. YOU DON'T!

the answers to everything, so it is absolutely vital that you know who your go-to people are.

The most detrimental pot-hole of all is one that can cause your operation to blow out the proverbial tire if not dealt with quickly and directly. Let me say up front that Nacogdoches did not deal with this issue, but I heard very specific instances of several other command centers throughout the disaster area that did. It is a virus that spreads quickly and infects without warning. Its symptoms seep through a group swiftly and sometimes, though not always, silently. Often borne of testosterone, we call this virus "Turf Wars".

Turf wars are uncomfortable, so no one likes to talk about them and often pretend that they don't exist, but as we found out, people will cease to function well, or even *leave,* an uncomfortable system. Turf wars have to be addressed directly even at the expense of personal ego. First of all, everyone must understand the importance of working as a team; all opinions are to be considered in order to gather a better perspective of the options available. If something isn't working, discontinue the methods and try another. It helps

> CLL – The "way we've always done it," may need to become "the way we used to do it." If someone else's ideas work, use them!

no one to be adamant about using a system that does not work. It cannot matter whose idea it is- if it works, use it. If it doesn't, then don't! Sometimes "the way we've always done it" doesn't fit the present situation and *needs* to become "the way we used to do it." Turf wars will blunt this move to focused group efficiency and teamwork if not dealt with quickly. Don't worry about who gets the credit – just get it done!

Several times during our recovery operation, I observed that officials from other state and federal agencies and even large metropolitan cities would visit our operation. They would tour our command center, sit in on a briefing or two with us, eat and then leave, never to be heard of again. Finally, after one set came and left, I became worried that something I had said or done had chased them away from the command center, so I approached a man on our leadership team with my concerns. I knew he had been attending briefings at the large area command center set up in the neighboring town and would have a better idea of what was happening. He broke out in laughter at my stated concerns of hurt feelings, and he informed me that the majority of these visits were basically gathering ideas from our operations. As liaison, he was then witnessing our actions being presented at the area command briefings as if the ideas were their own. I was excited! For our entire leadership team, progress was what was most important. We didn't care who used or modified what we were already making operational, so long as progress was moving forward.

A Turf War is a highly sensitive situation because it pertains to the human ego, but I cannot stress enough that it *must* be addressed. So what is a turf war? Turf wars occur when experts (real or perceived) will not allow for outside opinion. In other words, there are several different opinions at one time, but each has his or her own idea of how to handle the situation at hand. Team members are also unwilling to open themselves to constructive criticism and/or differing ideas. It creates constant tension and frequent battles when people cannot bend to the will of the greater good, instead clinching their fists tightly around their own agendas. Turf wars will limit the credibility of a disaster or crisis operation and holds the potential to crater your operation completely.

We ran into this concept of "turf wars" when people began showing up at our EOC from other command centers in the area. One particular

> **CLL** - Set the operational tempo early and often. That includes using words like "we" and "team." Intercept turf wars early.

set of government engineers left our command center after being informed that they were being reassigned to a different geographic location the next day. The next afternoon, I noted they were present in an afternoon briefing and later asked what had changed. It seems they returned to our EOC after finding their next assignment was a "testosterone swimming pool" and that you could "cut the tension with a knife." They simply refused to attempt to function in that environment and returned to our EOC because, "You guys are doing it right." A U.S. Congressman who toured the various operations in the area confirmed their attitude by saying that Nacogdoches had no turf wars and noting his surprise that leadership in other locations was allowing the inefficiency of the turf wars to continue.

During crisis and disaster operations it cannot matter to whom the credit is given so long as the efforts are successful. Too often as leaders we can lose sight of what our purpose is, and that is to help others. It is too easy to allow progress to be stunted by self-centered attention-seekers. It cannot be about the ego; it has to be about progress.

The final crucial element that only exacerbates the repercussions of the speed bumps, potholes, and detours is time compression. Especially during times of crisis, there is never enough time. Time is already a scarce commodity, but a disaster or crisis makes time shrink. Five hours might seem like twenty-five minutes and when someone decides to take a detour or become fixated on one issue, precious time is expended. We were being constantly inundated with information and data coming into the center. As a leader, I had to be aware of time but not fixated on how rapidly it was flying by. A leader must allocate time for planning, meetings, and working with individuals; he or she must also encourage others to do the same thing. Because time compression will force people to lose track of time, a leader must learn to regiment the schedule for the leadership team. Time compression is a catalyst for further frustration and chaos; therefore, it is necessary to be aware of the schedule.

This is a great deal of information for a leader to keep track of, but it is necessary to consider where your bumps, potholes, and detours are in order to prepare for them. For now, remember to expect distraction and at least a mild degree of fixation; be prepared to deal with them by setting clear goals through which to filter all information. Be ready to handle turf wars if you see them brewing; they must be nipped in the bud immediately. Finally, be prepared to handle all of the above under the crunch of time. Keep a level head and a clear vision of the big picture. Through it all, communication will be vital to helping your leadership team, staff, and volunteers work through the obstacles. Despite your best efforts to be clear, you will still find times in the midst of crises when you will say, "Is that what I really said?"

CHAPTER 5

Is That What I Really Said?

Further into the recovery operation, I began to conduct what is known as after-action interviews with personnel involved in the operations. These interviews were conducted with multiple people in the various agencies who had assisted in the crisis and covered a broad spectrum of technical assignments. The interviews involved a diverse group of disciplines from the sheriff and fire departments to the FBI, FEMA, and NASA. In every single one of the after-action interviews, communication surfaced as a major point of discussion and analysis. We had several positive reports, a few negative, but one fact was clear: communication affected *everyone* regardless of position. It was obvious throughout the operations that the worst pitfalls occurred when the basics of communication were neglected. Therefore, in crisis leadership clear, concise, well understood communication is second in importance

> **CLL**
> – Clear, concise communications in crisis is second only to the safety of the people.

only to the physical safety of everyone involved.

When reduced to its most fundamental purpose, the point of communication is to convey a thought or idea in such a way that another individual is able to fully understand. Anything else is a waste of time. Often, effective communication is lost because leaders are simply *going too fast*. Just as leaders set the operational tempo in physical operations, they must also set the communications tempo and expectations. Therefore, walk slower; talk softer. This is not a trite expression but rather an easily implemented strategy to bring calm to the chaos. People want to know in a disaster or crisis, "Is there any hope?" By setting an operational atmosphere that is purposeful but not rushed, the leader is saying, "Yes, it's tough; but we're all going to be okay. Let's focus our energies as a team to bring a good resolution."

Communication can easily be counted as the first thing forgotten or ignored until after an incident is over; by then, it is too late to repair the damage done. If effective communication is not exercised both during and after an incident, possible consequences include lack of closure on the part all team members, missing the identification of best practices through those situations that were successful, and lack of identifying the challenges and bumps in order to improve communication practices for the future. Through after-action debriefing, we were able to spot exactly where there were holes in our operation, how to improve our system in the future, and what methods worked best in the organizational process.

The bottom line for any effective communication is to KISS- Keep it Short and Simple. For the best results, communication must be reduced to the point of being ridiculously simplistic. It has been said that Napoleon Bonaparte achieved much of his success during the battles of the Napoleonic Wars of the early 1800's because his commanders consistently received explicit instructions from him during battle. Whenever Napoleon sent a message, he would whittle down the information until it was so basic that someone with "room temperature IQ," or lack of good sense, could repeat it back verbatim; only then would he dispatch that message. The messengers were strictly ordered never to add or subtract from the message. They were to deliver exactly and only what they had previously memorized. Napoleon's simple communication style reduced confusion in the midst of chaos. The same should be true in today's crisis communication but often is not. Simplicity in communication is vital; reduce it to the elemental.

There is one obstacle that every leader must anticipate when communicating information, and that is perception. A person's perception of events will heavily influence understanding in any situation. As previously stated, regardless of the facts at hand in a crisis, a

> **CLL – KISS** principle in crisis communications: **Keep It Short and Simple.**

person's perception is that person's truth for that moment in time. If you have ever arrived on the scene of an accident and asked two different eye witnesses to explain exactly what occurred as they saw it, chances are you received two different stories of varying degree. This is always an issue in times of crisis. During one of our regular EOC organizational briefings, I witnessed the potential conflict that differing perceptions can cause when trying to communicate.

We had one local law enforcement officer make a request that all entry onto private land in his area of the county be cleared through him. He had been getting complaints from the people in his area that searchers were entering and exiting at will, and it was causing high levels of anxiety. A shuttle structural engineer sitting in the room immediately spoke up and insisted that his crew absolutely needed to be the first to examine all debris; they could not risk any piece being moved or damaged by untrained personnel since each piece was vital to the re-creation and understanding of the events that caused the shuttle's demise. Therefore, his men needed the freedom to move about without delay. However, before he had finished speaking, the representative from the federal criminal defense investigative service interjected and demanded that *her* team be able to investigate each piece first because her agency was still trying to determine whether terrorism was the culprit in the disaster. There were three different perceptions, each equally significant, but unfortunately some-

> **CLL** – A person's *PERCEPTION* is his/her *TRUTH* in the moment, regardless of the *FACTS*. Work to establish FACTS as the common reference basis.

what obtrusive to one another. Each person had a unique need and was fully convinced that his/her perception was the truth we needed to be working with at the moment. Thankfully, we were able to finish the briefing and then later coordinate the needs of each individual. After taking them through the three pre-established recovery goals, we devised a method of search and recovery that satisfied each person. In working through this brief but tense encounter, I noticed several communication factors at play that further impacted the person's perception.

CLL – Linear thinker = detail oriented. **Spatial** thinker = broad pattern oriented. Both can help; both can hinder.

One such factor was whether the person was a linear or a spatial thinker. Linear thinkers are detail-oriented people. Oftentimes, they have difficulty getting "outside the box" and get caught up on any one unresolved detail whether pertinent or not to the overall issue. Often unable to see the whole picture, linear thinkers function better when they have all the pieces lined up in a row. Spatial thinkers, however, understand and communicate in broad patterns. More apt to see the grander scale, spatial thinkers simply need an overview of the whole to function well. Be careful, though, as spatial thinkers have the potential to overlook important details in pursuit of the broader picture. Linear and spatial thinkers complement each other, but they often do not communicate well together.

A leader must identify and bridge the communication gaps between linear and spatial thinkers. During our recovery operation, I encountered a retired US Air Force colonel who offered five powered parachutes to aid us in the search process. If you have never seen a powered parachute or heard of the mechanism, it is much like a go-kart with a large gas-powered engine, turning an airplane propeller, all located behind the rider; all of this is hung under a sport parachute. They generally travel very slowly, giving the rider the opportunity for a low and closer look at the countryside. Because we were having difficulty getting into several deep thickets to look for debris around our area, the idea of powered parachutes as a resource seemed both creative and rational. The colonel and I were communicating together in spatial terms; we each saw the opportunity as a creative solution to a difficult problem. During this time, however, the entire area was under an FAA no-fly order; therefore, no aircraft could be in the air unless it was military operated. I gave the colonel the name and contact information of the NASA Air Boss located at the area command center, and offered that Nacogdoches would be willing to employ the parachutes in a "test" run in the areas where we were having problems with ground searches due to dense vegetation. Soon after, we tested them in Nacogdoches County with excellent success. Only a few hours after we had flown the vessels, however, I received a phone call from another NASA official who was irate that we had flown the parachutes in the no-fly zone. It was obvious that a communication disconnect had occurred somewhere in the process, and the right information had not reached this person. Furthermore, the agitated official was obviously a linear thinker and had not received the details he needed to proceed comfortably with an outside-the-box solution. He was operating according to his responsibilities, so one cannot fault him for his concern when he called. However, it would have saved a great deal of time and grief had communication been properly transferred. Nonetheless, the Air Boss and I had been thinking spatially together and employed a unique solution for our unique problem; a linear thinker, as we found out, would need a little more detail to feel at ease. Almost like a brain, the synapses did not fire between the spatial and linear thinkers thus causing confusion, irritation, and difficulty. Once the proper connections had been made, it was a successful endeavor and all parties were pleased.

One tool has been found to be *most* effective in any communication, but specifically in crisis communication, and that is asking the right questions. What is meant by "right questions?" The vast majority of people will ask questions that begin with the word "why." Regardless of what follows that "why," people are expressing a desire to ask and understand, "Why did this happen to me?" "Why did this have to happen today?" "Why did this have to happen like this?" These are common questions when someone is emotionally distraught. Unfortunately, this line of questioning is self-defeating and useless because it drains energy, creates despair, and will generally escalate the crisis.

> CLL – Always ask the "right" questions. Right questions will bring useful answers.

Right questions seek to discover facts, outline potential solutions, and chart actions to possible remediation. Right questions empower; wrong questions overpower.

Right questions encourage; wrong questions discourage. Right questions will bring about focus, direction, and positive actions, whereas wrong questions can both prolong and intensify the crisis. When trying to gather information as well as when trying to verify that someone has fully understood communicated information, the best thing a leader can do is ask very clear and concise questions.

Oftentimes, a leader has to cull through the emotions and anecdotes to whittle information down to facts. Furthermore, once you have asked enough questions to feel comfortable that the bottom-line facts have been reached, it is a good idea to verify everything. Do not take any one person's word as the gospel truth until you have verified the information with another credible source, unless past experience with the person has established in you the highest comfort level with both their thinking style and communication ability. Use small words and short sentences. Small words can make a big difference in communication and will potentially aid you in giving and receiving only the facts. Remember, if understanding does not occur, then it is NOT communication!

Be sure to encourage your team members and staff to ask questions; in return, you as the leader must be receptive to any questions that will arise. Without being condescending, I would often find a way to have a person repeat back to me what I had just communicated. The purpose was two-fold: First, did they hear and understand what I

> **CLL – *FLASH!*** If the listener does not understand what you have said, it is **NOT** complete communication!

was asking or directing? Second, it gave me a chance to ask myself, "Is that what I really meant to say/ask?" Because the method was not demeaning, our entire team adopted this technique and found that communication was much more efficient as a result.

Another key factor in good crisis communication is personal knowledge of and trust in your key leadership team members. I would encourage any leader to either select a core team of leaders with which to surround himself or herself during times of crisis and get to know those people who you are sure will be a part of the process should something catastrophic happen. If at all possible, build and work with your team ahead of time so that communication borders on the intuitive. Look for people that are good at 'reading' others and communicating during times of stress and employ them in the processes. Learn to read people on your team quickly so that you can adjust communications when necessary.

It is never a good idea to fully judge a book by its cover, but at the same time, there will be tell-tale signs that will help you identify the personality and mental state of a person in times of stress. In the EOC we were very fortunate in that we had several people on the core leadership team who were great communicators, even under severe stress. One individual, a retired Houston Police Department officer, had years of experience communicating in times of crisis, reading people, and keeping everyone calm. He used his knowledge, training, and past experience to help all the groups performing the physical search for debris get "outside of the box" in their efforts. The Nacogdoches County Judge and County Sheriff were also capable of remaining calm during times of great stress and were able to efficiently and effectively communicate with diverse groups, organizations, and individuals. This was invaluable as they were the public faces of our operation, keeping the people in the county informed. I was fortunate to have one young lady on my team who had worked with me in a corporate setting before the shuttle disaster and understood both my communication and my thinking style. I quickly enlisted her assistance in the leadership team because she was able to communicate very quickly with me while keeping it short and simple. From past training, she helped me identify how people were communicating and basically served as my translator when I had difficulty understanding someone or communicating on an issue. She became an indispensable resource during that time and is a great example of why I cannot sufficiently stress the importance of having a group of efficient communicators on your team who can remain composed under intense pressure. This level of communicating will make or break your operation.

> **CLL** – During a crisis, communications must occur at all levels of the response, and not just at the leadership team level. It is the leaders' responsibility to make certain this is happening.

Until this point, I have discussed inter-personal communication because it is by far the most important, and often the most neglected, aspect during a crisis. However, there is one other facet of communication that our team found to be critical during crisis: from a structural standpoint, communication must occur at all levels. We had agencies and individuals responding from all over the country. It rapidly became vital for our leadership team to pinpoint who our liaisons were for each agency so that each was consistently well-informed on a constant basis. Should you ever find yourself working in a crisis situation with an agency that does not have a clearly designated liaison or representative, *you* supply them with one from your organization if necessary. Work to keep your liaison communication lines actively open until a rhythm on information flow is solidly established. I initially failed to do this, and the consequences could have been dire. In the first two days of the response operations, I felt as though I was constantly asking whether there had been hazardous material on board the shuttle for which my searchers needed to be aware and prepared. I could never secure a concise answer since I had yet to establish a clear liaison link with the correct authorities and organizations. Then, early one morning, I saw a TV news report that indicated the possible presence of yet-to-be-detonated explosive bolts that were for use on the shuttle's hatch. As I had been unable to establish a clear liaison link by this point in time, and since the safety of our personnel was now at stake, I made a call to my Congressman's aide to enlist his help in establishing this vital communication link. I could not take risks or wait on processes when the safety of our people was a concern. A few hours later, we received large posters listing all of the different potentially dangerous substances on board. From this point forward, I established who my liaisons were, or supplied the appropriate agencies with a liaison of my own and intentionally met with them on a regular basis so that I could remain properly informed and vice versa. I needed all levels of command communicating with me so that I knew exactly what the search teams were facing and how to best ensure their safety during the operation.

Everyone thinks he or she is able to communicate well; but until he or she has endured the grueling rigor of communication in times of crisis, he/she has yet to learn the full value and impact of efficient communication. Hopefully, you have gleaned three points from this chapter: Communication should be kept short and simple; it is not complete without reciprocal understanding; and when communicating, the leader must set the operational communication tempo-- walk slower and *talk softer.*

CHAPTER 6

IT'S ALL ABOUT PEOPLE

A leader must never assume that he or she must be the pivotal source of energy when leading any operation. If that occurs, the leader tends to forget that it is people who make up a team, and it is a team that makes things happen. Especially during disasters, volunteers come in all sizes, ethnicities, backgrounds, expectations, and abilities. This accumulation of people power comprises the many facets of the engine that runs the operation; a leader must make sure that all individuals are operating at full capacity and in the best position. Otherwise, the operations "vehicle" will inevitably have problems running. If someone is not in a position to best utilize or exercise personal strengths, a leader must have the stamina and tact to make the necessary adjustments. Simply put, it is common knowledge that a leader benefits from exercising good people skills; in times of critical incidents and disasters, the leader's people skills are a crucial factor in optimizing

CLL – People goal: right person + right place + right job

organizational response or reducing it to figurative rubble. Having learned from experience, I believe this a pivotal asset following closely on the heels of efficient communication. What are the necessary people skills a leader must employ?

A leader should be able to quickly assess the ability of an individual including his/her strengths, possible weaknesses, and functional capacity; then he/she must be placed where he/she can best assert his/her strengths. Because a disaster is not static but rather quite dynamic, strengths may become weaknesses over time and vice versa; therefore, a leader must be aware of how well each person's ability is being utilized. The leader must seek to set his/her people up to succeed. Conversely, the leader must be able to evaluate continuing personnel effectiveness based on two questions: Do the person's strengths still seem to be matched appropriately to the task? If a weakness is suddenly detected, is it a knowledge, training, or tools issue, or has the situation or task pushed the "strength" to the point that it is now a weakness? If a change in personnel is needed at this point, it should be facilitated quickly but compassionately. After all, the person being replaced may simply be physically fatigued and severely in need of rest. Remember, definitive action *with* compassion. As the incident evolves, so will the skills required to address the situation; this affects every aspect of a crisis operation from the physical methods employed to the personnel required to make things function.

Another key to helping a team succeed is determining the primary learning style for each person and then employing a communication method that most quickly and effectively communicates to that style. For instance, some people are kinesthetic learners and learn best though action, activity, or physical touch. Therefore, the best communication method may be to walk them through a specific scenario in order to help them fully grasp what is required of them. Other people are auditory learners and simply need to be told what to do before they can engage in the process. They hear it; they grasp it. Still others are visual learners and work best with a written list of expectations

> **CLL –** Learn to spot learning styles quickly. Visual, Aural, Kinesthetic. Communicate to reach all styles.

and requirements, or even a picture drawn on a board or paper. Everyone has some ability in each of the three key learning styles; everyone also has a dominant method that best suits them which is what we as leaders are looking for. The quicker and more effectively team members learn, the more rapidly they can be set into action. There were times during briefings that I would hand out a written record of each meeting, talk through it, and then walk through any part of it that I could in order to reach each learning style. My goal was to work all three learning styles at one time. Learning styles are considered by some to be mere nuances, but in the heat of disaster, if these nuances are overlooked, the ramifications can be huge.

While searching for the "best people" to fit each role, it is crucial to remember that the person with the most credentials may not be the best player for your team. He/she may have superb skills, training, and past experience, but may also be the biggest disaster to ever hit your team if his/her attitude and ability does not mesh with the rest of the team. Sometimes, position and credentialing are nothing but a set of useless letters and titles; some of my best resources during the shuttle recovery operations were people who had little to no formal education or training but could think outside of the box and accomplish the task at hand quickly and efficiently. The best thing a leader can do when getting a team together is to look for creative solutions to the unique situations he or she will face. Seek the right person for the right job at the right time.

> **CLL – Seek positive team members.**
> There are times when positive ATTITUDE is better than APTITUDE (skills.)

Inevitably, there will be personalities that will clash within your team; it would be foolish to believe otherwise. However, the best way to make people work well together is to lead by your actions and become a servant, setting an example of excellence in demeanor and actions. As a rule, people will want to help someone else if it is felt the person can be trusted, and trust is built through service together. As a leader, make it a habit to regularly look at your crisis from "1,000 feet higher," always keeping the larger picture in view. Do not dictate or mandate, but personally demonstrate to your team how they should operate: work with them, not above or against them.

This will help you as the leader to better serve your people.

Consider that as a leader, you are building a people "tool box" to work with during disasters. You are searching for the best tool (person) for the job and are trying to keep the tool sharp and safe for use. When working with tools, however, there is always a certain tension over the power about to be released through the use of the tool. Am I being safe? Is the tool right for the job? How quickly can I accomplish this job using this tool? That tension, along with many of the same questions, is similar to the kind one might experience when working with people under stress, and it will sometimes bring out reactions the leader must be prepared for. Oftentimes, people will not realize that when they encounter tension, it is simply a case of personality difference or unwillingness to bend the knee to help another person. Leaders must monitor their people for signs of this friction, silently observe the interaction, and then move to intercede quickly if the "tools" appear as though they will "bang into" each other. One discipline that will help leaders identify potential difficulties between team members is having a working knowledge of the different personality types that people exhibit. What do I mean by this?

Behavioral scientists, psychologists, and counselors have written volumes on the subject of personality types and traits. In my own library resources, one chart I have matches the different definitions and

> **CLL -** People are the leaders "tools" to work with. Know how they work, how to care for them, and how to keep them sharp.

nomenclatures of personality types that have been published throughout previous decades; the total is well over two dozen. Of the many personality descriptions published, the four most commonly are labeled Choleric, Melancholy, Sanguine, or Phlegmatic. Understanding each type, the key traits and outcomes, and the impact that has on a person's performance is immeasurably helpful to a leader in times of crisis response.

CLL – Choleric = strong, forceful, commanding.

The Choleric is a person whose personality is more like that of a military commander; he/she treats leadership with a command and control mentality. Generally dominant, strong, decisive, and driven to get things done, the choleric person is much like a lion in the animal world. When they roar, they want everyone to listen! Cholerics are often referred to as the "natural leaders" as they do bring drive, focus, and energy to any operations. Unfortunately, they can often be stubborn, arrogant, and abrupt in dealing with others; furthermore, the choleric is definitely not the personality to bother with fine details. Someone with a choleric personality must learn to tame the abruptness in order to harness the full power and strengths that personality type exhibits.

CLL - Melancholy = systematic and detailed.

A strong Melancholy personality is the person who is more analytical or systematic in actions. He/she typically spends a significant amount of time and energy thinking, assessing, making lists, evaluating, and analyzing everything. Much like the beaver in nature, this person is especially skilled in keeping up with the details of the leadership or operational team. Additionally, he/she can be cautious by nature, have difficulty with rapid change, and prefer thoughtfully devised

> **CLL**
> – Phlegmatic
> = caring, considerate, loyal.

written plans. Can you see, already, where conflicts could arise just between team members with only these two personality types? But wait, there is more!

A Phlegmatic personality can be the source of unusual strengths and challenges in any team. Phlegmatics are much like golden retriever dogs in the animal world; they love everyone and are good at making friends. Very loyal, caring and considerate, these people seek steadiness and a peaceful resolution for everyone. Great empathizers, Phlegmatics are excellent at serving others in leadership but may struggle with giving strong, decisive directions

> **CLL - Sanguine =**
> fun-loving, spirited, excitement oriented

as a leader. After all, they just want what is the best for everyone.

Finally, there is the Sanguine personality. The strong sanguine person is spirited, active, and loves to have fun which is much like the otter in nature. As a matter of fact, if it is not fun, then the activity is certainly not ideal for them. This is where a sanguine person struggles in leadership, for leading in times of disaster is certainly not fun! The great part about the Sanguine person, though, is the amazing amount of influence and dynamic energy that person brings to the team. They have a way of connecting with others that the choleric personality just does not understand.

Everyone has a little bit of each of the four personality types listed above, and almost everyone has a greater tendency towards one of the four. Despite a dominant personality style, however, anyone can learn the skills and needs of the other personality types. Through personal experience in multiple disasters, I have observed that in times of crisis, specifically during the personal and organizational tension the crisis fosters, people tend to gravitate to the characteristics of his/her dominant personality type. The leader will then function out of the strengths and weaknesses therein. Effective leaders watch for this and seek to synergize the strengths while neutralizing the weaknesses.

For instance, it has been my observation that those with melancholy personalities are quickly caught up in the disaster details too much while the sanguine has a tendency to exhibit everything from inappropriate humor to personal meltdown because the ordeal is so intensely serious. At the same time, and hopefully at appropriate moments, the sanguine is the person who brings much needed comic relief during intense briefings or meetings. The phlegmatics in the operation sometimes let the weight of the emotional overwhelm them, even to the point of having to be removed from the operation for rest and recovery. However, they are outstanding at sensing the emotional and psychological state of fellow team members, sometimes spotting a personal "meltdown" before it can occur. And what of the cholerics, the lions in the team? Though extremely helpful in directness in the early stages of an operation when safety and action are paramount, they can later become outright annoying because they lead by telling others what to do rather than leading by example. There are times when they are not serving anything but their egos.

Personalities aside, leaders working with teams of people in times of crisis or disaster must be able to mentally be in two places at the same time. First, leaders need to always keep the "big picture" view of the entire operation. By observing current personnel patterns, leaders can anticipate the impact that time compression, distraction, and fixation will have on individual members. Secondly, leaders also must have a pulse of what is going on at the ground level of the team. Who is stressing from strain? Who has not rested properly? Who needs encouragement? Who needs redirection? By understanding the personality types and traits, leaders can more quickly be at both "places" of leadership, more effectively assess team needs, and more fluidly help the personality traits of each team member mesh with others as a team.

> **CLL –** Dominant personality style. Everyone has one, so discover what it is quickly and work with it to synergize team actions.

Another people factor often overlooked in the rush of disasters is learning to delegate authority. Monitor the progress, yes, but you must delegate authority, and when you do, stand behind that delegated leader in the decisions he or she makes. On one morning during the first week of our response operations, the unit leader of the DFW airport team leader for that day approached me with the news that he had removed a person from the DFW mobile command post. It seems that the party involved, though a wonderfully intelligent and well meaning man, was nevertheless taking actions and making demands considered inappropriate to the operations of the workers in the mobile command post. It was obvious that this team leader was a bit nervous about passing along this news, but I very calmly looked at him and said, "That's fine." Taken aback, the leader looked at me and asked, "Really?" After re-assuring him that he had every right to do as he saw fit for the progress of the operation, he said something I will never forget: "You know, I can follow you." I did nothing special, other than supporting the decision of the team leader. In doing so, I again reminded myself that not only did I have to be willing to delegate authority, but I had the responsibility to monitor the situations and support the system our leadership team had set in place. Personalities had clashed, and the necessary adjustments had been made appropriately. It was time to move on.

One sidebar comment I would make at this time is that even though the material regarding people in this chapter was identified and classified during the shuttle Columbia disaster, these key points have been validated in numerous disasters both by myself and other leaders I have visited with over the past thirty years of emergency work. Communication styles, thinking styles, and

> **CLL –** The leader must always keep the big picture, or situational awareness, at the forefront of his/her consideration.

personality types are all topics of which leaders must be constantly aware, and must be willing to make the appropriate changes when necessary.

Finally, a leader must be conscientious of all that we have discussed previously and all activity that is going on without being a micromanager. Because the leader's job is the hardest in that he or she must prod all of the "troops" to march in step in the same direction, it is not unusual for frustration to override self-awareness. Strive to be cognizant of the small things in your interpersonal communications such as tone of voice, inflection, and body language. Once again, as tired as you may be of hearing this by now, you as the leader are setting the operational tempo with every action you take and every word you speak. If you want a smooth operation, set a smooth tempo.

It is a fine balance a leader must learn to live: diving into the dirty and getting sweaty alongside the teams, all the while keeping a keen observing eye on the entire process from the "1,000 feet higher" perch. Observant and fierce as an eagle, yet caring and nurturing as a shepherd, the leader must cover all the bases in caring for team members and associates. After all, it's all about people.

CHAPTER 7

Got Style?

"You know what? I finally figured out what drives me crazy about the way you function in disasters," one woman on our leadership team said to me one afternoon. "Whereas I can handle the chaos if I can segment it into manageable bites – you just thrive on bringing order out of total chaos!"

Every leader has a style of leadership. Normally, the leader's style is derived from a collection of experience, training, whether formal or informal, perceptions, thinking style, personality type, communication style, natural talents and probably another half dozen factors not mentioned. In fact, talking about a leader's style is similar to talking about regional language differences in the United States. We all speak English, but our accent, or dialect, may differ from region to region which can cause communication issues between people from two different areas of the county. In difficult situations, language can make all the difference for communication and progress. What people do not often like to accept is that different styles of leadership can have huge impacts on two main disaster components: communication and progress.

In traditional business models, many people have been fortunate enough to work for the focused, calm leadership style that encourages and brings out the best in a team. This leader is able to take a tough business situation and verbally paint a vision for the team that is non-threatening and uplifting, yet still calls for direct action. The result is that this team usually exceeds the set goals and has a great sense of fulfillment in doing so. There are other business leaders, however, who are just the opposite and the results are usually disastrous. This negative, often tyrannical leader may still push the team to reach the stated goals, yet destroy the morale and future functional viability of the team in the process. Team members do everything they can to leave the team as soon as they have opportunity. Both positive and negative leaders have a specific style, and both heavily impact their team under normal conditions. However, during times of crisis, the style of leadership will have an even greater, more immediate impact on the type of outcome produced.

After the experiences gained through the shuttle Columbia disaster and other large-scale disasters since, I have found that during times of crisis there are three predominant leadership styles that, regardless of training, people will have a tendency to employ. Each leader will have one style to which he or she will default, but it is imperative to learn how to effectively engage with the other two for optimal team performance. The three styles are command and control, consultative, and collaborative, at times also referred to as consensus.

> **CLL – Command & control leadership. Forceful, authoritarian, direct.**

The military approach to leadership best describes the command and control style. The leader gives orders; others execute them. There is no opportunity given for idea interaction, and it is the "leader's way or the highway." This style is an absolute necessity when imminent danger or safety issues threaten lives on the team or when other operational issues dictate immediate action. However, if not used appropriately, it can isolate the leader from the team thereby eliminating the opportunity for interactions that would be profitable to the operation. It can also pit the team against the leader, creating barriers that can be devastating during a quick-paced crisis operation. Former military personnel

> **CLL – Consultative leadership. Team interactive, best-practices approach prior to final decision.**

and strong choleric, or lion type personalities tend to use this style more frequently because it is something that past experience has engrained in them.

Consultative leadership is a style in which the leader is constantly looking for the best practices to solve issues or problems at hand. The leader *actively* seeks the ideas of everyone on the team, within reason, to find the best solutions and the best methods of implementation. In the consultative style, the leader must make the final decision, but he or she actively interacts with the team to ensure that everyone has a voice. The goal is to establish that there is validity in everyone's ideas, and to encourage others to expand on the suggested ideas. The final authority is still the leader's, as well as the responsibility for the decision; but the leader also knows that people will support what they help build. Even if a team member's idea is not used, the member at least feels he/she had a part

> CLL – Consensus leadership. Group rule and decisions.

in the final decision. The weakness of the consultative style is that it may take too long, depending on what is happening at that time. Additionally, the leader must be able to identify only the best practices and not try to please everyone with the decision he/she makes. The consultative style requires that the leader be able to actively listen, discern what is helpful and what is not, and to carefully choose his or her words in response to all ideas.

In the consensus style, the leader passes the decision-making process over to the group. He/she then becomes simply a facilitator, and the team as a whole becomes the decision-maker; in theory, majority rules. The leader must make the team members keenly aware that because they are making the final decision, they also carry the responsibility for the outcome. There are potential benefits of this style in that it creates personal investment in the progress of the operation as a whole because each person has a voice in building it. Weaknesses include the fact that the process may result in a team divided, especially during a crisis when emotions are high, fatigue is inevitable, and personality differences are decidedly evident.

During times of crisis or disaster, a leader may need to employ all three leadership styles at different times during the same operation. Furthermore, it may be necessary to shift quickly from one to another depending on the circumstances. As stated earlier, command and control is more appropriate when it comes to issues of safety or in the early stages of a disaster when the leader has to make rapid decisions and has little time for discussion or input. This style is usually a necessity when the leader needs to quickly create order out of chaos. If you as a leader find yourself defaulting to this style for a period of time out of necessity, it is imperative that you continually ask yourself the right questions as discussed previously in chapter five- "Is That What I Said?" Since you are not enlisting other input in this style, your decisions had better be the correct ones.

During the shuttle operations, I employed all three styles of leadership at one time or another. For example, I arrived at the EOC within twenty minutes after the first shuttle piece struck the ground and became Incident Commander due to my position within the county as Homeland Security Director. No one who would soon be on my leadership team had arrived, and there were hundreds of incoming reports of debris pieces falling to the ground at that very moment. Nothing like this had ever happened, and I had no experience on how to secure a shuttle crash sight. At that point, my main concerns were for the safety of the people on the ground, and whether there was anything hazardous that the people responding to the incident would encounter. Furthermore, I was searching for solutions as to how to keep people indoors until we were sure the sky had stopped falling.

Second only to the concern for safety was my concern for what to do with the debris once it was found. Previous experience with aircraft accidents had taught me that outside agencies would want to be able to re-create the incident using the pieces left from the crash. Relying on that previous experience, I knew that we needed to determine a way of securing each piece of debris; therefore, I decided to get my resources moving in the right direction and made a command decision to have the law enforcement, Texas National Guard, Volunteer Fire Department personnel and other first responders protect each piece as best they could. In these first moments, time necessitated command and control leadership.

Once things settled down and the leadership team came into place, it was more prudent for me to use a consultative style of leadership. I knew that I did not have all the answers, but that with the collective experience and training of the people on our leadership team and operational personnel, answers would be found. I then became the facilitator of discussions and made the final decisions when appropriate; but I relied heavily on our team for input and ideas. Each member of our executive leadership team handled their responsibilities in much the same way. It was imperative that we obtained correct and helpful information to make informed decisions. Now that safety was not the main issue, it benefitted us to have the people working in unison with us to help "build" the entire operation so that the team would want to support it. Once again, people will support what they help build, particularly in times of crisis.

> **CLL –** Listen to the team for ideas...ALL the team. Some of the best answers may come from the least likely people.

Perhaps the greatest strength regarding the consultative style of leadership is that it is not intended to appear to be hierarchical to other team members; this will often create a very open, free flow of ideas as solutions are sought. During the shuttle response operation, some of the best ideas came from clerks, dispatchers and volunteers who were all pooling ideas from years of experience handling different situations. Everyone must have a voice at the table of consultative leadership, and everyone certainly did during the Nacogdoches portion of the shuttle response.

In one situation, the manager of the Nacogdoches Exposition Center, who was also acting as the search operation liaison at the EOC, was working with the volunteer groups who were daily going out into the field, searching for debris. At one point he approached me with the information that his team had changed from a reactive mode to a more pro-active approach in the search for shuttle debris. Instead of waiting for reports of debris to be funneled to their search teams, the teams were now beginning to actively look, mark, recover, and clear specific areas in a disciplined manner. This occurred after this team leader asked his team members for ideas for better ways to address the search process. Numerous people gave suggestions about using maps, map grids, GPS equipment, and other ideas. After quickly reviewing the input, the search leader made the decision to employ geo-spatial grids of the county, search each grid spot, and mark it as cleared with visual indicators on the ground as well as on the map so that they would not double back in their process. There was even a local surveying company that shut down company operations for over a week so that their surveyors could assist with the search. The surveyors would coordinate the maps with surveying flags to clearly mark the edges of the map grid coordinates for the search teams. This enabled the searchers to target areas where they had previously not searched due to thick underbrush while at the same time not wasting time and energy by accidentally moving off course. This method provided a more manageable and efficient means of working the search and recovery process, particularly in the early, chaotic stages. When the manager informed me of the changes, I could tell that the decision had been coordinated and well-defined. Therefore, I asked a few simple questions regarding any unintended consequences and then felt comfortable encouraging his team to continue full-force.

There was rarely occasion during our particular operations for the consensus leadership style due to time constraints, but occasionally it was a helpful method. Near the end of our recovery operations as a county, when things had slowed considerably, we had time to make decisions as a group on issues of less severity. In disaster and crisis operations since the Columbia, I have noted all three leadership styles in operation, and observed validation of the strengths and weaknesses as previously listed above. Note that it is normal, in times of pressure and stress, for a person to revert to his or her predominate style of leadership. Regardless of what he/she has previously tried to learn, it will always be true that as human beings, we tend to revert to what makes us most comfortable.

Personality type weighs heavily on leadership style, which is why it is important to both understand your own personality type and be able to quickly and accurately identify types on your team. For example, if you know you are a strong choleric (or lion) personality type, you may discover that you naturally return to command and control, even if you know you should really be using a more consultative approach at the time. Someone with a more phlegmatic (golden retriever) personality type might find himself/herself fixated and distracted with concern over the human suffering; as a leader, he/she would more than likely have a tendency towards consultative or consensus styles of leadership out of desire for everyone to "feel the love." A sanguine (otter) personality will almost always choose consensus over any other type of leadership style. He/she, as the socialite and fun-loving, will want everyone happy with the decisions made all the while making light of anything possible in order to break the tension. Sanguine personalities tend to shy away from conflict and responsibility, instead opting to keep everyone in good spirits. When they do take a balanced leadership style approach, however, they are perfect for keeping things "light" in the midst of serious issues. The leader with a melancholy (beaver) personality has an enormous tendency to micromanage everything on the team, thus becoming bogged down and overwhelmed, rather than delegating. He/she might attempt to use a consultative style but will always tend to gravitate towards the command and control style. To this leader, the purpose is to account for every last detail.

Any leader can train himself/herself to quickly shift between the three leadership styles discussed. It starts, however, by making the conscious decision to be aware of all the various factors playing into the issues influencing leadership style, and knowing his/her personal communication style, personality traits, and thinking type. Additionally, it doesn't matter what style of leadership a leader uses so long as he/she does not try to know and do everything alone. A good leader relies on resources, finding people that are capable and empowering them to do the jobs for which they are qualified. The only thing left is to make sure that everyone has the appropriate tools to do the job well and to keep obstacles out of their way.

> **CLL –** Leadership style is a choice. Choose to be a flexible leader by using all styles.

Other than the shuttle Columbia disaster, I have found through at least two other large regional disasters that I can confirm two things for the reader: First, leadership really is about style. Second, the leadership styles you employ will enhance or hinder the entire team's efforts. So what is your leadership style?

CHAPTER 8

THE DEVIL IS IN THE DETAILS

You want to know what this chapter is really about? It is about the part of any operation that most leaders don't like to discuss – details. It has been said before, "The devil is in the details." At no other time is this saying truer than in the midst of a crisis or disaster. Whether it is a family tragedy, a company crisis, or a regional disaster, leaders must pay attention to the details of an operation. Note that I did not say "fixate" on details; just make certain the details are properly addressed.

Throughout the shuttle Columbia disaster response, we discovered the importance of covering all details on several occasions. I recall one specific time when I dropped this "details" ball in a big way. From an earlier chapter, the reader will recall that the DFW Airport Mobile Command vehicle arrived in Nacogdoches County early on day one of the disaster. Our leadership team initially put DFW's extensive electronic capabilities to use handling the flood of incoming telephone calls regarding shuttle debris. A day or so later, due to the ever expanding disaster response scope, we divided the debris tracking between the DFW crew and a second crew established in a separate motor home brought into the EOC parking lot. One afternoon, the Sherriff and I received a report that our debris call receiving/logging operation was facing a growing backlog of calls that were not being followed up in a timely fashion. In short, all of the reports about the location of debris were being lost in a communication void, never being confirmed by our personnel nor mediated or picked up by retrieval crews. Immediately, I went to the team who was dealing directly with the phone calls and asked what I thought were the right questions; I even received some pretty good answers. We discussed options of quick changes to the process and I left the center thinking the problem had been satisfactorily solved.

The leadership team received a follow up report a few hours later informing us that the backlog of calls was still growing. The Sherriff, along with another member of the leadership team, went to the group and made further inquiries as to what was happening. The difference this time, however, was that the Sheriff took the time to have the team go into great detail and physically show him exactly how they were handling the calls step by step. In taking the questioning to that level, the Sheriff soon discovered the root cause of the slow down, modified the process on the spot, and the challenge was solved. The backlog of calls began to decrease markedly from that point on. This incident served as a clear reminder to me that the devil really is in the details. Ask more questions, if necessary, to be certain problems are mediated quickly.

The great challenge for any leader in dealing with details is the delicate balance that must be maintained between leadership facilitation and leadership fixation; giving direction versus getting distracted. In the military, leaders talk about how battles will sometimes ebb and flow – high intensity at one moment followed by hours of boredom. The same can be said for disaster but in another sense. High-energy intensity at one moment may be replaced with "breathing room" a few hours later only to be followed by a sudden return to "battle tempo" as some new incident or concern unexpectedly surfaces. Throughout all of this, someone must still be taking care of the details.

For Nacogdoches County, another challenge that demanded the management of details involved dealing with the vast number of people who were spontaneously traveling to our county to be a part of something historic and volunteering to help. Some were motivated to come out of a sense of duty or patriotism, others out of sheer curiosity, while still others were sent by the emergency agency they worked for on a daily basis. Few came prepared to shower, feed, and provide personal shelter for any length of time, and our leadership team quickly found we needed to be in the sheltering business. Thankfully, three different national organizations that specialized in mass feeding came on the scene and helped feed the volunteers. Our Exposition Center team cleared out an area in a large room there at the Center where cots and sleeping bags could be set up, while still other visiting volunteers set up camp on the grounds outside. The people were a blessing to our manpower needs, and also a challenge if considering the details commensurate with supporting them. At this point I must interject the fact that when it comes to handling details regarding physical or resource needs, the Incident Command System (ICS), mentioned earlier, provides a framework for dealing with this on a consistent basis. Regarding support structures, in would be to any leaders' benefit to become familiar with the components of ICS.

Dealing with details can become a necessity in many different facets of the disaster. Here are just a few major areas, along with general questions we had to deal with during the Columbia operations. If you are a person who might one day find yourself in a position requiring attention to details in a disaster, begin to think about the following questions and how they might impact your operation.

Human resources:

1. Are our people safe? Is everyone accounted for?

2. Do our people have the equipment they need to be safe in the environment in which they are working?

3. Are our people self-sufficient in their basic needs, i.e. food, water, and shelter? Is everyone prepared, or do we need to supplement any supplies?

4. Based on the present expected time for the operations, will we need additional personnel? If so, where will we acquire them?

5. If additional personnel are en route, when will they arrive, where will we stage them, and what are their expected equipment needs?

6. How and where will we check the people in, how will we track them, and do we have planning in place for keeping up with people after they have checked out?

7. Do we have an easily identifiable telephone number for family members to check on their loved ones who may be assisting with the operation?

Physical resources:

1. Do we have enough food, water and other necessities to feed everyone who needs a meal?

2. If not, where can we acquire what is needed and how soon? Local suppliers? Local organizations?

3. Do we have enough equipment for the length of time we think the operation may take, such as generators, lights, flashlights, batteries, appropriate protective clothing, gloves, eye protection, and other items for safety or use?

4. Do we have a process in place to maintain equipment that may need quick repairs? How will we track that?

5. What projected needs do we have in the next eight hours, twelve hours, twenty four hours, and seventy two hours?

6. Where will we stage our equipment and supplies such that everything is accessible but also secure?

Fiscal resources:

1. Are we tracking all expenses for possible reimbursement later?

2. Who is responsible for tracking this and do they have the tools they need?

3. How are we authorizing and verifying purchases?

4. Is everyone in the field of operations totally informed on purchasing processes and spending guidelines?

5. Do we have enough cash on hand to deal with any purchases that need to be made in cash?

6. Do we need to contact our financial institution to utilize any prearranged financial instruments? Who has the authorization to do that?

Legal:

1. Does our legal team have all the information it needs to be ahead of the curve in anticipating any legal actions we need to execute?

2. Is our legal team monitoring all operations for possible areas of liability?

These questions represent just a few of the hundreds of details that may arise during crises or disasters, and the leader(s) must make certain all points are being addressed. Though I have touched on this before, I'll say it again: A leader must always be looking and thinking outside of the box, especially regarding details. Do not be afraid to transfer useful lessons from past experience and employ them in the present situation to facilitate problem solving at the detail level. For instance, when I worked in one corporate world job, I used to hate having to deal with process flows. However, in the midst of the shuttle Columbia response, I found myself using written process flows on numerous occasions to either anticipate potential problems, or to solve the problems at hand. I would even sketch everything out on a whiteboard when necessary, just to make certain I was not missing a small but crucial point. Be aware of the details!

What is the best way to deal with details? Lists. If your personality style is anything but Melancholy, you probably let out a small moan at the word "lists," but that is the most comprehensive and finite way to deal with details. Start your disaster detail lists now while there is no crisis, time is plentiful, and there is no pressure from an expanding incident. Use the questions mentioned previously as starting points, and then add everything you can think of. There is no detail too unimportant when it is the crucial one. By the way, do not for a moment think that lists like this are only good for business, government, or the military. In my family, we have a "disaster check list" that each member keeps in his/her vehicle. It gives the steps to take in communicating with family, finding shelter, and ensuring everyone's safety after a large disaster. In this way, my family members are equipped to make calculated and concise decisions based on the steps listed on the card. Furthermore, they are prepared to fend for themselves if circumstances require. If a disaster or crisis occurs, you may very well be the person acting as leader for the moment, either formally or informally. It is better to think through the small points now before a crisis hits. Please, believe me when I say that I have learned from experience that the devil really is in the details.

CHAPTER 9

STOP THE PRESSES!

"Bob, when you get a moment, you _must_ take a look out the back door and see the parking lot! You will not believe what it looks like!" said one of the people on our leadership team in the EOC. The "it" they were speaking about, I soon discovered, was the virtual sea of media satellite uplink trucks parked in packed precision on the parking lot and lawn of our EOC. It was an unbelievable site, if one had never seen it before; most of us had not.

When the shuttle Columbia tragedy began to unfold on February 1st, we knew the press would be heavily involved, and they were. What we discovered over time, though, is that the media was both our best friend and our greatest challenge. Thankfully, they were a problem only rarely. From the beginning of the tragedy to the closeout of the Nacogdoches EOC, we worked to integrate the needs of the media with the needs of our operation as seamlessly as possible. We learned from them, and they learned from us. From our experiences with media, we discovered that the vast majority of reporters were hard-working, well-meaning people who had a job to do – report the news. To be sure, most of them did it with their "slant" on the news. There were a few, however, as there are in any profession, who not only were troublesome but also created unneeded havoc. They were the small minority, and over time we realized who they were and tried to keep them somewhat isolated from the operation.

One of the key issues that any leadership team or individual leader must realize is that a disaster or crisis will take on a life of its own in the media if media relations are not handled well. In the midst of the crisis, you may release well-worded, concise press releases only to open the paper or turn on the TV and see a report that has you scratching your head and wondering, "Now where did they get THAT false information!" We found it does not have to be that way, and as a whole it was not a problem for us during the Columbia disaster. Remember, media personnel have a job to do, so work to help them, and they just may surprise you how much they can assist you. There are a number of "Do's" and "Don'ts" that we used and found helpful.

First, appoint a designated Information Officer (IO) or designated organization spokesperson as quickly as you can. This person should become the one and only source of information coming from your organization or group—period! Remind everyone else on your team, from the top leader to the lowest ranked team member, that there is one media contact point. If planned correctly, this IO will be a person who has either a media background or who has had previous training in media relations during disasters. This is a crucial point as your organization's chief officer may not be the person best suited to stand in front of the press. Sometimes even the most ardent media trainers cannot rid a key leader of that deer-in-headlights look. In such cases, the key leader might be put to best use behind the scenes. Nevertheless, whoever speaks has to make their words count. The media contact needs to be calm under stress (set the operational tempo!); he or she must be somewhat articulate and "media savvy."

Next, be honest. Tell the truth and never lie. This does not mean you have to give out every bit of information you are asked for, but professionalism should rule the day. Never say "no comment." Instead say, "I don't know, but I will try to find out for you," or "I am sorry, but that information is not available at the moment." During the first four or five days of the shuttle recovery operations, our chief elected officials, the county sheriff and the county judge, were constantly bombarded by the media for any information regarding the status of the lost astronauts. Frankly, the media was in a macabre feeding frenzy at one point regarding the lost astronauts. Finally, our County Judge held up a piece of paper on which were the names of the lost astronauts. With firm grace, she informed the press present at the briefing that the list of names she held represented human beings who had been tragically lost to the NASA family, and we would NOT be party to any discussion regarding their status. And we did not.

Organize key messages and prepare a brief script prior to meeting with the media. It helps both your leadership team and your IO to stay focused and not be drawn off message.

In today's media environment, always think and speak in terms of sound bites and headlines. Sound bite news is what is going to come out of any media briefings you will conduct so make certain your printed media release provides input into what those sound bites and headlines will say. This also means your key points need to be in short sentences in your media release. Remember the chapter where we discussed communicating in disasters, especially the part about keeping your communications simple? That is an absolute necessity in your media release.

Speak slowly and clearly when you or a member of your team addresses the press personally. Be prepared not only to clearly state your name but also to spell it. Be aware of your speech pattern and speed; inflection and tone of voice can often send unspoken messages that were never intended. When addressing the media, either as an IO or as a key leader, you will certainly want to enforce the personal discipline to "walk slower; talk softer." Just as in the rest of the crisis, strive to set the operational tempo of the media briefings.

Coordinate messages within your leadership or command structure. Make certain that there is a free flow of information within the organization prior to making it a public commodity. Your team members and/or other associates should hear major news from the leadership team first, rather than hearing it from a public broadcast source. Otherwise, team morale and cohesion can be damaged. Let your people hear it from the key leaders first.

Offer printed hard-copy background information to the media, along with a printed copy of the main points you will bring out in your media briefing. However, do not be surprised if your information is misquoted. During the first week of the shuttle recovery operations in Nacogdoches County, our leadership team was giving a media briefing approximately every two to four hours of every working day. Though we practiced each lesson previously listed including the "hard-copy" point above, you can imagine our confusion when we would run across an occasional article that contained a large number of factual errors. It became a game for us to sit in the EOC each morning with several regional and national papers at hand, and compare the published stories in the papers to the facts on the written briefing sheets handed out at the media briefings the day before. Wow! Where did they (the news media) get some of that stuff!?

Along with the "Do's" of working with the media during disasters, there are also several areas of which your leadership team will do well to steer clear. For instance, **never use irony or sarcasm.** It will make your leaders seem flippant, uncaring, or out of control and will most definitely come back to haunt you later, either in the media or in a court of law during a lawsuit.

Never speculate. See point number two above, "be honest," if you are not certain what I mean by never speculate. Regardless of how many caveats or conditions you place before, during, or after your speculative statement, it will still be portrayed as iron-clad fact complete with your name attached. It is so much easier to say, "I'll get back to you with that information when becomes available." This honesty is much less painful in the process.

Never use alarming words that may cause anxiety. Once again, address facts and not emotions and <u>set the operational tempo</u>, which means use words that calm and give hope. It will pay dividends not only at the moment but also in the long run of the operation.

At this point, you may be asking yourself, "Just what do I need to tell the media?" Use the following list as your guide to developing your own comprehensive media briefing form:

1. Who are you?

2. What has happened? Remember—be factual, not inflammatory.

3. Is anyone hurt?

4. Is there any danger to people or the environment at the moment?

5. How will the public be notified if they should do something, like taking shelter, evacuating, etc.?

6. What steps are you taking to control the situation?

7. What is your greatest concern right now?

8. Is there any disruption to traffic or other services?

9. Who else can the media or the public contact for information? This should be the IO or a single key leader. Give a phone and email to the media.

10. Once again, never use alarming words that may cause anxiety.

Remember, the media has a job to do; the more you and your leadership team can help them in effectively accomplishing that job, the better the results for everyone. The fact remains that over-zealous reporters exist. During the Nacogdoches shuttle operations, one such reporter kept pestering local law enforcement officers to take, show, direct, drive, or in some way deliver him to a piece of space shuttle debris for a personal picture session. He was convinced that we were covering up news in some way and wanted to circumvent the media process we had set in place.

Finally, in a quiet display of personal frustration, the officer relented and began to give the reporter very detailed directions to an area of the county where, he assured the reporter, there was shuttle debris that no one had yet found! In his zealousness, however, the reporter missed the mischievous glint in the officer's eyes and immediately drove off to find his treasure trove of unreported news. What the reporter did not know, was the area he was being sent to was so remote, so rugged, and so physically foreboding that there was a standing joke in the Sheriff dispatch area: if you have to send a deputy to that area on a call, also send a wrecker to pull the deputy's car out!

To this day, we are not certain what happened to the reporter. He never appeared at another media briefing; he never called 911 for assistance, and he did not even fire a distress flare over the pine trees!

CHAPTER 10

(NOT) FOR CHRISTIANS ONLY

At the outset, let me give fair warning regarding this chapter. It deals with the faith aspects of a disaster and is therefore overtly, unashamedly religious in nature. Furthermore, it has a distinct Christian slant as both the author and the overwhelming majority of the Nacogdoches leadership team members that worked through the shuttle Columbia disaster are practicing Christians. If that makes the reader uncomfortable, then you may want to skip this chapter and go on to the next. If, however, you are a person of faith, Christian or otherwise, or you are curious about the part faith can and does play in times of disaster and crisis, I urge you to read on. For the Columbia shuttle disaster, faith was a quiet but important bedrock that both supported and guided everyone involved through very difficult days.

Defining moments seldom enter life with urgency or fanfare. Often, they slip by quietly. Only in retrospect do we recognize that we have experienced a defining moment--not so on February 1, 2003.

With the loss of the space shuttle Columbia over the skies of Texas, a defining moment came roaring to life. While it was a sad moment for the US space program, it was also a defining moment revealing that faith sustains people in times of disaster. For the majority of us working the entire process, it was also a reminder that God does indeed honor the practice of faith displayed in the prayers of his people.

Psalm 15:1-2, deals with intent of the heart elegantly yet directly. *"O Lord, who may abide in Your tent? Who may dwell in Your holy hill?* (NASB*) *He who walks with integrity, and works righteousness, and speaks truth in his heart."* At the time of the shuttle disaster, it was common knowledge that a large portion of the NASA astronaut community was composed of men and women of faith. They neither flaunted nor paraded their beliefs but quietly lived them in their daily quest for professional excellence. The people who responded to East Texas on that fateful day in 2003 were no different in their desire to honor God through excellence in word and deed.

The most precious faith discipline that God honored throughout the entire shuttle recovery effort was that of prayer. Our corporate prayer life began at a leadership meeting on the afternoon of February 1, 2003. Operations had reached a frenzied pace already, and people were beginning to show signs of stress.

In an effort to regroup, I called the leadership of all organizations represented in our command center to a separate sequestered meeting. We gathered in a conference room for a moment of seclusion to refocus our thoughts and actions. Before we could start, however, our County Judge, a devout woman of God, pointed out that we simply were never going to make it through this tragedy on our own. We had to go to God, the source of power, guidance and strength. With the simple words, "Let's pray," we all bowed our heads as she led us in that first leadership team prayer. It was simple, elegant, and powerful.

That first prayer began a discipline of prayer that started and ended each day's work in our emergency operations center from that point on. I later found out that prayer was also the prelude each day at our staging area located some blocks away. There, hundreds of workers joined hearts before God in prayer prior to departing and fanning out to search for debris in the dense brush and thorny thickets of East Texas. Were they Baptists? Methodists? Episcopalians? Presbyterians? Catholics? Who knows? Religious titles had no meaning at this time.

The common need to pray to God was all that mattered; and God honored those prayers. Want to hear about the stormy weather that miraculously skirted around our county at one point during a crucial time of recovering debris? That was no chance of nature—it was the power of prayer. Safety? That was prayed for every day. Only scratches from brush were reported as injuries. Guidance about what to do next? Prayer always seemed to bring answers that were successful. Leaders prayed. Rescue workers prayed. Prayer warriors prayed. Homemakers prayed. Children prayed. God honored those prayers in myriad ways.

God also honored the integrity and diligence of those who participated in the recovery operation. On numerous occasions, I had workers and officials from agencies outside Nacogdoches comment on the professional, friendly, and helpful demeanor of the citizens and workers in our county. In maintaining Godly integrity in interactions with people under pressure, a chaotic situation never dissolved into a frenzied atmosphere.

Since that tragic day, there have been ceremonies of remembrance each year on the anniversary of the shuttle disaster, and I hope we will always honor the seven lives that were tragically lost that day. But more so, I hope we will remember that the shuttle Columbia disaster was also a time when God honored his people, their faith, and their prayers.

Scripture quotations taken from the New American Standard Bible, Copyright © 1960, 1962, 1963, 1968, 1971, 1972, 1973, 1975, 1977, 1995 by The Lockman Foundation Used by permission. (www.Lockman.org)

EPILOGUE

A paraphrase of Proverbs 22:3 from the Bible says that when we see danger approaching, if we are smart, we will prepare for it. If we are not, we will suffer for our lack of preparation. If past trends are any indication, disasters will continue to grow in complexity, geography, and intensity in the United States in the coming years. Competent leadership will be needed from the top executive to the head of a family to lead successfully through the crisis. Decisions will be made during those times of crisis and disaster that will affect lives; as leaders, we must prepare now to function well during those times. Our decisions will be crucial and impacting. Right choices can save lives; poor choices can leave people injured or dead. We must equip ourselves so that our poor choices are few and far between.

The great challenge in writing this book has been in the vast number of points that I wanted to cover versus the time to do so. It is a challenge to help people in positions of daily authority (or leaders) to understand that the leadership skill sets employed for leading during and through disasters are somewhat different, and that management, no matter how it is framed, is not necessarily leadership. People accomplish tasks assigned by managers; leaders encourage people to "rise to the next level" of excellence with directed encouragement.

Now that you have read through the book, I ask you to make a second reading, but this time with a pen in hand. Look at every part of the book with these questions foremost in mind, "Where do I fit within this information, and what do I need to do to move forward in a positive manner? What do I need to learn or change in order to more quickly and positively influence people to take action, to be a leader?" As you answer these questions for yourself, make notes in the margin, or capture ideas on paper. The end result may very well be a new action plan to challenge and enlarge your personal leadership skills. Do it quickly, though. Do not wait until the sky is falling around you.